D1243558

UNITED NATIONS CONFERENCE ON TRADE AND DEVELOPMENT

INVESTMENT POLICY REVIEW

GHANA

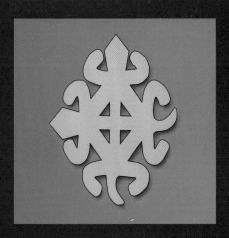

UNITED NATIONS

UNCTAD/ITE/IPC/Misc.14

United Nations Conference on Trade and Development

Investment Policy Review

Ghana

UNITED NATIONS
Geneva, June 2003

Note

UNCTAD serves as the focal point within the United Nations Secretariat for all matters related to foreign direct investment and transnational corporations. In the past, the Programme on Transnational Corporations was carried out by the United Nations Centre on Transnational Corporations (1975-1992). UNCTAD's work is carried out through intergovernmental deliberations, research and analysis, technical assistance activities, seminars, workshops and conferences.

The term "country" as used in this study also refers, as appropriate, to territories or areas; the designations employed and the presentation of the material do not imply the expression of any opinion whatsoever on the part of the Secretariat of the United Nations concerning the legal status of any country, territory, city or area or of its authorities, or concerning the delimitation of its frontiers or boundaries. In addition, the designations of country groups are intended solely for statistical or analytical convenience and do not necessarily express a judgement about the stage of development reached by a particular country or area in the development process.

The following symbols have been used in the tables:

• Two dots (..) indicate that data are not available or are not separately reported. Rows in tables have been omitted in those cases where no data are available for any of the elements in the row;

• A dash (-) indicates that the item is equal to zero or its value is negligible;

• A blank in a table indicates that the item is not applicable;

• A slash (/) between dates representing years, e.g. 1994/95, indicates a financial year;

• Use of a hyphen (-) between dates representing years, e.g. 1994-1995, signifies the full period involved, including the beginning and end years.

Reference to "dollars" ($) means United States dollars, unless otherwise indicated. Annual rates of growth or change, unless otherwise stated, refer to annual compound rates. Details and percentages in tables do not necessarily add to totals because of rounding. The material contained in this study may be freely quoted with appropriate acknowledgement.

INVESTMENT POLICY REVIEW SERIES

1. Egypt

2. Uzbekistan

3. Uganda

4. Peru

5. Mauritius

6. Ecuador

7. Ethiopia

8. United Republic of Tanzania

9. Botswana

10. Ghana

PREFACE

The UNCTAD Investment Policy Reviews are intended to help countries improve their investment policies and to familiarize governments and the international private sector with the investment environment in these countries. The Reviews are considered at the UNCTAD Commission on Investment, Technology and Related Financial Issues.

The Investment Policy Review of Ghana was initiated at the request of that country's Ministry of Foreign Affairs and the Ghana Investment Promotion Centre (GIPC). In preparing the Review, UNCTAD received the full support and cooperation of the Chief Executive and staff of GIPC, the Government of Ghana and the Permanent Mission of Ghana to the United Nations Organizations in Geneva.

The views of the international donor community in Ghana, the international private sector and domestic business were canvassed at various stages of the project.

The report benefited from the contributions of experts within and outside Ghana. The national experts included George Manu and Peter Morton of Empretec Ghana, and research assistance was provided by Kessewaa Brown. Comments were contributed by Colin Roberts and Jacob Saah. The international experts included John Gara, Dato Jegathesan and Todd Moss.

The UNCTAD staff included Diana Barrowclough, Khalil Hamdani, Fiorina Mugione and Zbigniew Zimny. Rory Allan, Mongi Hamdi and Joseph Mathews also provided inputs. Signe Krogstrup, Lang Dinh, Riad Meddeb and Mike Pfister provided research assistance. Elisabeth Anodeau-Mareschal and Virginie Noblat-Pianta provided production assistance.

The United Nations Development Programme provided funding for the project.

It is hoped that the analysis and recommendations of this Review will contribute to an improvement in policies, promote awareness of investment opportunities and serve as a catalyst for increased investment in Ghana.

Geneva, February 2003

CONTENTS

ABBREVIATIONS

AGOA	-	African Growth and Opportunity Act (AGOA)
ACP	-	African Caribbean and Pacific
AGC	-	Ashanti Goldfields Corporation
BIT	-	bilateral investment treaty
CEPS	-	Customs, Excise and Preventive Services
DTT	-	double taxation treaty
FTZ	-	free trade zone
ECOWAS	-	Economic Community of West African States
EU	-	European Union
FDI	-	Foreign Direct Investment
GDP	-	Gross Domestic Product
GFCF	-	gross fixed capital formation
GFZB	-	Ghana Free Zones Board
GHIA	-	Ghana Ports and Harbours Authority
GIPC	-	Ghana Investment Promotion Centre
GIS	-	Ghana Immigration Service
GSP	-	General System of Preferences
HIPC	-	Highly Indebted Poor Countries
ICSID	-	International Convention on the Settlement of Investment Disputes between States and Nationals of other States
IPP	-	independent power projects
MEST	-	Ministry of Environment, Science and Technology
MFN	-	Most-Favoured Nation
MIGA	-	Multilateral Investment Guarantee Agency
M&As	-	Mergers and Acquisitions
NEPAD	-	New Economic Partnership for Africa's Development
NGO	-	non governmental organization
ODA	-	Official Development Assistance
PPP	-	purchasing power parity
REPA	-	regional economic partnership agreements
R&D	-	Research and Development
SMEs	-	small and medium-sized enterprises
SOE	-	State owned enterprise
S&T	-	science and technology
TNC	-	transnational corporation
UNCITRAL	-	United Nations Commission on International Trade Law
VRA	-	Volta River Authority
WTO	-	World Trade Organization

GHANA

Key economic and social indicators GHANA

INDICATOR	1991	1999	2000	2001*	2002*
Population (million)	15.1	18.8	19.2	19.7	20.2
GDP at market prices (billion of current dollars)	6.6	7.8	5.0	5.3	5.8
Annual GDP growth (percentage)	3.3	4.4	3.7	4.0	4.3
Inflation (percentage)	37.3	12.4	25.0	33.0	13.8
Total Debt (percentage of GDP)	66.4	90.2	133.6	126.2	..
Debt Service (percentage of exports)	27.1	20.8	19.1	15.3	..
GDP by sector (percentage):					
• Agriculture	45.5	35.8	35.3	35.9	..
• Industry	17.0	25.4	25.4	25.2	..
- Manufacturing	9.3	9.0	9.0	9.2	..
- Services	37.5	38.8	39.3	38.9	..
FDI inflows (millions of dollars)	20.0	63.0	114.9	89.3	..
Exports of goods and services (percentage of GDP)	17.0	31.9	49.2	52.2	..
Imports of goods and services (percentage of GDP)	25.5	49.2	69.6	70.5	..
Gross domestic investment (percentage of GDP)	15.9	21.0	23.7	24.0	..
Human development index	0.5	0.5	0.5	..	..
Aldult illiteracy rate (percentage of people aged 15 and above)	70.5	30.0	29.0	27.0	..

Sources: UNCTAD, FDI/TNC database, *World Bank, World Development Indicators,* 2001, UNDP, *Human Development Report,* 2001, Economist Intelligence Unit, 2003.
*Data for 2001 and 2002 are provisional. GDP figures reported by the Central Bank of Ghana in billion cedis are as follows: 20,579 in 1999; 27,152 in 2000

INTRODUCTION

Ghana is making a comeback in terms of attracting FDI. An African front-runner in the mid-1990s, Ghana slipped into economic crisis in 1998 and has only recently begun to recover. A renewed sense of purpose and optimism emerged following the country's peaceful transfer of power and the first new political leadership in 20 years. The new Government has pledged to create "a golden age" for business through private sector development, regional integration and good governance. This resolve is being well received by investors, and FDI inflows have picked up to pre-crisis levels.

The immediate challenge is to broaden and sustain the recovery. For this, a stable macroeconomic environment is a priority. Recent policy efforts have resulted in inflation and interest rates being significantly reduced, but the levels are still too high for normal investment activity. Also, measures are needed to revitalize domestic enterprise activity in the main sectors. These efforts should support poverty reduction actions under way, especially in the Northern, Upper East and Upper West regions.

The main aim of FDI strategy in the immediate future should be to encourage existing investors to reinvest in Ghana's economy. New investments by existing foreign investors in mining, agribusiness, telecommunications and financial services are expected to contribute to the increase of employment, exports, foreign exchange receipts, tax revenues and economic growth. A "booster programme" is recommended to regenerate domestic and existing investor initiative. Reinvestments will encourage new foreign investors to enter Ghana.

In order to sustain the recovery, longer-term measures will also be required. Chapter I shows that FDI trends were uneven before the present economic crisis. Ghana has never experienced a stable inflow of investments - in spite of a long tradition of openness dating back to the early years of independence. Sustained FDI inflows in the future will require an investment environment that enhances the competitiveness of business and of the Ghanaian economy as a whole.

There has been no recent reform of the investment framework; chapter II suggests that there is room for improvement. The Investment Code, which in 1994 was considered the best of its kind in Africa, needs updating. In addition, bottlenecks in company incorporation, labour laws, access to land, tax regime and administration need to be cleared of obstructions. Policies in key sectors – mining, tourism and agriculture – should be fine-tuned and brought in line with investor requirements. In particular, the Mining Code does not compare well with the framework provided by new alternative FDI locations, such as the United Republic of Tanzania, where Ghanaian mining firms are now important outward investors.

Chapter III outlines Ghana's FDI potential and the strategic directions that are needed to tap it. With the right policies in place, FDI may be attracted in the long term by:

◆ A revamped privatization programme. Telecommunications and power appear to hold further potential for FDI if the policy and regulatory environment can be improved while ensuring that benefits from privatization are more widely shared than in the past;

◆ Infrastructure development through the private sector. The capital investment requirements for infrastructure-upgrading are huge and can be eased by private project financing; and

◆ A reinvigorated Gateway strategy (a comprehensive trade facilitation programme, see box III.5) to remove supply constraints to export-oriented manufacturing for markets in Europe, the United States and the rest of Africa.

A central theme is that private sector development is essential in order to attract and benefit from FDI in the long term. There is a need to promote business start-ups and small and medium-sized firms, to encourage the formation of linkages between local firms and foreign firms, and to build enterprise capabilities generally - including the promotion of education and science and technology policies that are responsive to the needs of the private sector.

The Government should strengthen the institutions for private-public sector dialogue and the institutional links to enable the Ghana Investment Promotion Centre (GIPC) to act as a "one-stop centre". Investment generation and servicing should be GIPC's core activities, geared to encouraging enterprise clustering in key sectors and providing institutional support and advice to both local and foreign investors.

Chapter IV highlights the main conclusions and recommendations for an agenda that should be shaped through dialogue with all stakeholders and implemented by the Government in close partnership with the private sector.

I. Trends and performance

One of the main aims of the Government of Ghana in recent years has been to instil confidence among investors and create an attractive environment for foreign direct investment (FDI). Ghana was among the first countries in Africa to pursue economic reforms. Yet FDI trends have not been sustained, and Ghana has not been able to reap the benefits that a more stable inflow of investments could bring.

A. Recent investment trends

1. FDI size and growth

Ghana has a long, though modest, history of FDI. The early foreign establishments date back several centuries. In more recent times – the 1970s – FDI was mainly in import-substitution manufacturing. Annual inflows were as high as $68 million for about two years, but were much less in most years, even slipping to negative numbers (net outflows) in the late 1970s, and hovering at under $5 million in the mid-1980s, (figure 1.1). With the introduction of the Economic Reform Programme (ERP) in 1983, Ghana undertook a relatively successful transition from an administrative system of economic management to a market economy. Gross domestic product (GDP) grew at an average annual rate of 5.4 per cent between 1984 and 1990 and gross fixed capital formation (GFCF) doubled as a percentage of GDP[1]. FDI remained sluggish in the years immediately following the start of reforms, accounting for less than 1 per cent of GDP. However, it soon picked up, and during the period 1991-1995, Ghana was considered a front runner, ranking among the top 10 investment locations in Africa.

Figure I. 1. FDI flows to Ghana, 1970-2001

(Millions of dollars)

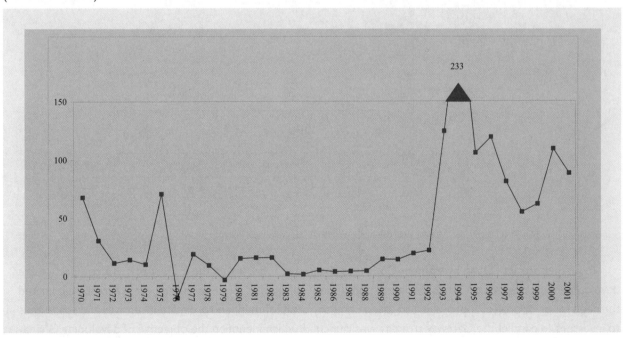

Source: UNCTAD, FDI/TNC database.

---

[1] Gross fixed capital formation (GFCF) as a percentage of GDP rose from 5.2 in 1978-1983 to 10.8 in 1984-1990. E. Aryeetey et al. (2000). *Economic Reforms in Ghana: the Miracle and the Mirage.* Oxford, James Currey Ltd.

The increase in FDI was triggered by the adoption of policies in 1986 to attract investment in natural resources. Investor response to the new mining law enacted in 1986 was positive, causing a surge of investment similar to a mini "gold rush". The divestiture programme also attracted FDI. When privatization began in 1988, there were 350 State-owned enterprises (SOEs), many of them unprofitable. The programme had a slow start, and in the first round of divestitures, only 55 SOEs were privatized while another 31 firms were liquidated. A turning point came in 1994, when the Government put its most prized asset, Ashanti Goldfields Corporation (AGC), on the market. Consequently, 1994 saw an abrupt peak in FDI flows of $233 million, reflecting the partial sale of AGC to the South African mining company, Lonmin. This deal, one of Africa's largest privatization to date, put Ghana in the spotlight for international investment. FDI also flowed to services. Among another six divestitures in 1994, were those of Accra Breweries and Standard Chartered Bank. The most recent peak of FDI inflows was registered in 1996 when Telekom Malaysia bought 30 per cent of the shares of the then State-owned Ghana Telecom.

Figure I. 2. Africa: top 20 countries for FDI inflows, annual average for 1992-1996 and 1997-2001[a]
(Millions of dollars)

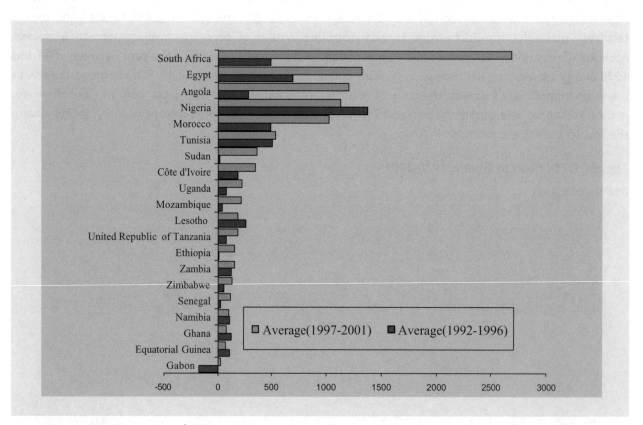

Source: UNCTAD, FDI/TNC database. [a] Ranked on the basis of 1997-2001 inflows.

To further attract FDI, an Investment Code was enacted in 1994, within the framework of a comprehensive development strategy: Vision 2020. The Investment Code – praised at the time as the best in Africa – eliminated the need for prior project approval; it also eased company establishment and provided incentives and guarantees to investors. In parallel, the Gateway strategy was launched, which identified the objective of developing Ghana as a regional investment hub by "attracting a critical mass of export-oriented firms to kick start export-led growth as well as facilitate trade by removing the constraints to the development of exports and investment".[2] However, Ghana's front-runner status proved short-lived. After 1996, FDI inflows declined and Ghana barely just made the ranks of the top 20 FDI recipients in Africa in 1996-2000 (figure I.2). Many of Ghana's neighbours – such as Senegal and Côte d'Ivoire, which attracted less FDI than Ghana in 1991-1995 – have had a comparatively better experience in recent years.

Relative FDI indicators, adjusting for size of economy, also show Ghana's recent performance to be weaker than that of neighbouring countries and similar resource-based economies (table I.1). FDI flows to Ghana in the second half of the 1990s were less than those to the United Republic of Tanzania, a least developed country that has consistently ranked lower than Ghana in terms of attractiveness and which initiated economic reforms and opened up to FDI much later. In an attempt to revive investors' interest, the Government announced in 1998 a new phase of the divestiture process. But expectations were not met, as the Government had already divested full and partial stakes in its largest banks, mining, manufacturing and service companies. Ghana, competing with other emerging markets for capital, faced difficulty in finding strategic buyers for its remaining assets, mainly in public utilities. The benefits of privatization were also questioned. The Government's relationship with the largest privatized company – Ashanti Goldfields – was strained, which had implications for foreign investor perceptions of Ghana's privatization programme (see box I.1).

Table I.1. Relative FDI performance in selected African countries, 1992-2001

(Millions of dollars and percentage)

Country	ABSOLUTE PERFORMANCE						RELATIVE PERFORMANCE					
	FDI inflows		FDI Stock		FDI inflows per capita		FDI inflows				FDI stock (Dollars)	
	Millions of dollars		Millions of dollars		Dollars		Per $1000 GDP (Dollars)	As per cent of GFCF			Per capita	Per $1000 GDP
	1992-1996	1997-2001	1992	2001	1992-1996	1997-2001	1991-1995	1996-2000	1991-1995	1996-2000	2001	2000
Ghana	121.4	80.9	358.0	1 346.8	7.2	4.3	17.4	13.4	8.1	5.9	68.2	242.3
Botswana	- 32.5	69.4	1 299.6	1 733.7	- 25.2	45.8	- 12.1	14.3	- 5.0	6.0	1 115.5	363.2
Côte d' Ivoire	186.3	351.9	1 063.0	3 684.9	13.1	22.6	13.4	33.5	13.5	23.2	225.4	365.8
Nigeria	1 374.8	1 126.1	9 680.9	21 288.6	14.2	10.2	47.5	34.4	31.4	13.6	182.1	491.3
Senegal	26.0	119.3	272.4	977.3	3.2	13.0	3.1	21.1	2.5	11.2	101.2	194.9
South Africa	490.5	2 684.3	10 657.5	50 114.7	12.2	62.6	2.9	10.8	1.7	6.8	1 144.4	345.2
Tunisia	506.9	533.3	8 447.7	11 671.6	58.0	56.9	30.6	25.7	11.5	10.3	1 220.6	588.4
United Republic of Tanzania	76.1	186.1	104.7	1 403.9	2.5	5.4	10.2	21.3	4.4	13.3	39.0	130.7

Source: UNCTAD, FDI/TNC database.

---

[2] Source: World Bank (1998). Press release No. 99/1874/AFR.

However, the main deterrent to new FDI was the deterioration in economic conditions. In 1998 and 1999, Ghana's economy suffered a shock with the fall in prices of its major exports – cocoa and gold – and the rise in price of its major import, oil. Severe trade imbalances, a rapidly depreciating currency and high interest rates, accompanied by an expansionary fiscal policy, yielded unsustainable budget deficits.[3]

Economic performance was also affected by an electricity crisis caused by droughts. Power shortages are estimated to have reduced national output by 4 per cent in 1998 and a further 1 per cent in 1999. FDI inflows recovered in 2000. The policies introduced by the new Government, which took office in January 2001, have helped stabilize the economy. A restructuring of debt under the Heavily Indebted Poor Countries (HIPC) programme is taking place. In addition, major efforts are being made to see that recent improvements in living standards in the Accra and Ashanti industrial regions will also be felt in other much poorer regions and sectors of the economy.[4]

Foreign investors are also likely to be reassured by the strong pro-business attitude of the new Government – which has promised a golden era for business. But the decline of worldwide FDI in 2001 has deterred inflows to Ghana as elsewhere. Domestic factors, such as progress in the establishment of a regulatory framework governing privatization, improvement of the internal economic environment, revival of the Gateway strategy and regional integration can play an important role in cushioning the adverse effects of the global downturn in FDI and, in the longer term, restoring Ghana to the ranks of Africa's front-runners.

2. Sectoral distribution

Investors are attracted by Ghana's wealth of gold, aluminium, bauxite, timber, diamonds, manganese, and oil and natural gas exploration. Around 70 per cent of all FDI is in natural resources. FDI in manufacturing is mainly resources-based, such as the processing and export of cut pineapples to European markets and the processing and canning of fish. In services, foreign firms play an important role in banking and in the construction sector, building roads, public works and hotels; most of these activities are financed by some combination of public funding and development assistance. Most recently, there has been an increase in FDI in the energy sector.

The Ghana Investment Promotion Centre (GIPC) provides information based on registered projects – excluding energy and mining – outside the free zones. As of December 2002, the GIPC had registered 410 projects in the services sector, 387 in manufacturing, 165 in tourism, 111 in building and construction, 116 in agriculture and 204 in trade. These projects, of varying size, comprised 966 joint ventures with Ghanaian interests, and 427 wholly-foreign-owned projects, and are estimated to account for a total of $1.5 billion of foreign capital. 70 per cent of registered projects have been implemented. The pattern of FDI in the main sectors is discussed below (see also table 1.2).

---

[3]   Additionally, the frequent recourse to the short-term domestic debt market to finance the fiscal deficit has resulted in significantly high inter-est rates, leading to the "crowding out" of the private sector from the credit market. The independent Centre for Policy Analysis (CEPA) in Accra concluded: "Ghana's current economic problems, in a fundamental sense, have their origins in the lack of complementarity between fis-cal and monetary policies. (Centre for Policy Analysis, *Ghana Macroeconomic Review and Programme*, Accra, CEPA, 2000: 41).

[4]   Republic of Ghana "Ghana Poverty Reduction Strategy", Progress Report 2002.

(a) Mining and energy

Mining accounts for the lion's share of total FDI in Ghana, particularly for aluminium, bauxite and manganese, although the main industry centres around diamonds and gold (Ghana's Obuasi goldmine is the second largest producing goldmine in Africa, after the one in South Africa) (see annex I, table AI.I).

A distinct feature of mining in Ghana is that the Government retains a 10 per cent free share with an option to acquire an additional 20 per cent in mining ventures, thereby maintaining managerial voice in these firms. This limitation does not appear to have deterred FDI. FDI in oil exploration began in 1996 but has yielded few results, and new measures are being taken to revamp foreign investor interest.

Ghana relies on hydroelectricity for its power needs. The State-owned Volta River Authority has encouraged private investment from independent power producers. Large projects to expand capacity at existing plants and develop new ones involve international companies such GE Hydro, CMS and Marathon Power of the United States.

Table I. 2. Sectoral distribution of investment in projects registered by the GIPC, 1994-2002*

(Millions of dollars and percentage)

Sector	Inward Investment (Million US$)					Percent of total FDI				
	1995	1996	1997	1998	1994-2002	1995	1996	1997	1998	1994-2002
Agriculture	1.41	0.33	0.69	1.23	203.96	8.26	2.97	1.02	6.04	11.52
Building & construction	0.25	1.87	0.86	2.24	125.90	1.47	16.85	1.27	10.99	7.11
Export trade	0.38	0.10	0.12	0.13	15.63	2.23	0.90	0.18	0.64	0.88
General trade	0.80	2.77	17.54	6.78	101.25	4.69	24.95	25.85	33.27	5.72
Liaison office	0.04	0.05	0.00	0.01	0.10	0.23	0.45	0.00	0.05	0.01
Manufacturing	6.86	3.29	5.71	4.92	345.64	40.21	29.64	8.41	24.14	19.52
Service	6.93	2.13	42.34	4.50	944.37	40.62	19.19	62.39	22.08	53.32
Tourism	0.39	0.56	0.60	0.57	34.21	2.29	5.05	0.88	2.80	1.93
TOTAL	**17.06**	**11.10**	**67.86**	**20.38**	**1 771.06**	**100.00**	**100.00**	**100.00**	**100.00**	**100.00**

Source: GIPC database, figures represent actual transfers as communicated by the Bank of Ghana and the Ghana Customs; Excise and Preventive Service. *Note: Investment in oil and mining are excluded.

(b) Manufacturing

There is FDI in food, aluminium and plastic products, and foreign participation in non-traditional agribusiness export industries also appears to have been strong. Among the leading examples of FDI are the Pioneer Food Cannery in Tema, which is partially owned by United States-based Heinz, and the cocoa-processor, West Africa Mills in Takoradi, which was bought by a German company following privatization. Other major firms are in food manufacturing and distribution: Ireland's Guinness Ghana Ltd., Germany's Ghana Agro Food Company, Coca-Cola Bottling Company, Accra Brewery Ltd., and other well-known names such as Cadburys of the United Kingdom and Switzerland's Nestlé Ghana Ltd.

Box I. I. Ashanti Goldfields Company Ltd.: maintaining a golden share?

Ashanti Goldfields Company (AGC) is Ghana's single most prominent company. Operating since 1897, it holds an important position not only in the economy, where it produces more than half the national gold output, but also in the national psyche. It is the leading share on the local stock exchange, with a market capitalization of around 2,392 billion cedi;[5] and in 1996 it was the first company from sub-Saharan Africa to be listed on the New York Stock Exchange.

AGC remains the most visible source of Ghana's presence in the international economy; for many investors, AGC is Ghana. This perception persists despite the fact that AGC is increasingly becoming a pan-African company, rather than relying solely upon Ghana where it has continued to play a key role in generating exports, providing employment and income. It produced 1.7 million ounces of gold in 2000, two-thirds of which were in Ghana alone (other mines are located in Guinea, the United Republic of Tanzania and Zimbabwe). It continues to employ more than 10,000 people, despite some job losses after closing uncompetitive open-pit mines, and its wages are significantly higher than the national average. It is the largest corporate taxpayer after Valco (see box III.3) and the largest source of foreign exchange earnings after Cocobod. ACG also stands out as an example of the changing relations between the government in Ghana and the private sector. It was first listed on the London Stock Exchange in 1897, and has produced gold almost continuously since then, regardless of the many ownership changes. In 1968 Lonrho (the parent of Lonmin) took over the company and it became a private concern. By 1994 it was 45 per cent owned by Lonhro and 55 per cent by the government, although the Government's share was reduced to 20 per cent after the privatization sales. Lonrho took a 32 per cent share, and the rest was held by various shareholders, including some major international financial firms. Shares are now listed on six stock markets, providing an important link between Ghana and international investors. Recently there have been tensions in AGC-Government relations, which could have significant implications for perceptions of Ghana's investment environment. Failed hedging strategies nearly pushed the company into liquidation in late 1999, and this, combined with a public and personal conflict between company officials and top political leaders resulted in a severe deterioration of investor confidence. The share price fell sharply, leading creditors and shareholders to demand major changes. The new administration is seeking to repair both Government-company relations and investor confidence, including a public willingness to consider further divestiture.

Source: UNCTAD survey.

(c) Services

The services sector (infrastructure, tourism and trade) attracts smaller volumes of FDI by comparison with the other sectors, but accounts for the largest share of FDI in registered projects. Construction and tourism are examples where foreign companies play a lead role. The United Kingdom construction company Taysec, for example, which has operated in Ghana since 1947, has been involved in constructing hotels, roads and other major infrastructure projects. Recently, FDI in telecommunications accounted for the largest share of FDI in services and also triggered new opportunities for services-related FDI in remote data entry operations. Another area with a significant foreign presence is banking. Some foreign banks have been in Ghana for a very long time: in particular Barclays and Standard Chartered, which have histories in the region dating back a few hundreds of years. However, FDI in banking was not significant until after the 1983 reform programme, after which two additional private merchant banks entered in 1990 plus one commercial bank in 1991. There are now 17 foreign banks in Ghana, and a number of leasing companies, two savings and loans companies, a venture capital company, a finance house and a mortgage company, in addition to two discount houses.

---

[5] *Source:* Ghana Stock Exchange, August 2002.

3.   Sources of FDI

The sources of FDI have varied over the past few decades. Traditionally Europe, and especially the United Kingdom, were the largest sources of FDI flows to Ghana, mainly into mining and other resource-based activities. South African investors now play a major role in the mining industry. They also focus on domestic market opportunities, particularly in brewing and the distributive trade. Interesting recent developments are signalled by GIPC data. As shown in figure I.3, Asian investors account for the largest investment in registered projects: for example, China, India and Malaysia were increasingly important in the recent bout of privatization. Malaysian companies have invested substantially in the telecommunications and telephone sector, including television and film, infrastructure and the provision of services for the free trade zone. The television station, TV3, and the film group, GAMA, are both Malaysian-controlled; and when Telekom Malaysia purchased 30 per cent of the shares of the then State-owned Ghana Telecom in 1996, it accounted for the largest share of FDI flows that year. However, in 2002, Telenor of Norway has been appointed to replace Telekom Malaysia as the manager of Ghana Telecom.

In terms of number of projects, the United Kingdom was the single biggest investor, accounting for 10 per cent of the total (146 projects), but it ranked only fourth by investment value after Malaysia, the United States and Switzerland (figure I.4). Ghana also has a large number of foreign investors from India, Lebanon and Syria, who serve the domestic and tourist markets through general trading, import-export and the hospitality sector.[6] The presence of Asian investors in Ghana is the result of the GIPC's investment promotion programmes.

Figure I. 3. Ghana. Distribution of FDI in registered projects by region, 1994-2002*

(Millions of dollars)

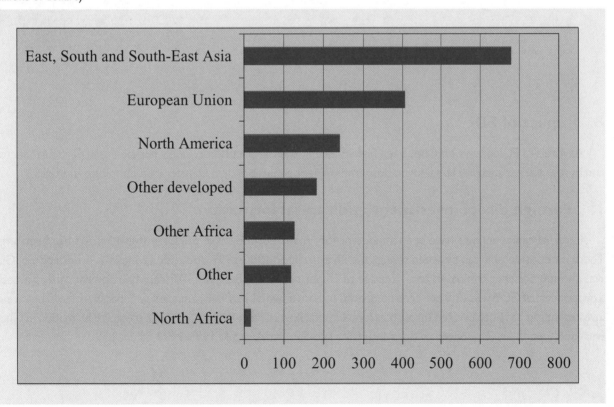

Source: GIPC, Ghana. * FDI in oil and mining are excluded

---

[6] The Ghanaian Indian Association directory, for example, records the presence of about 1 000 Indian firms in Ghana.

Figure I. 4. FDI in registered projects by country of origin: the top 10 investors in Ghana, 1994-2002*
(Millions of dollars)

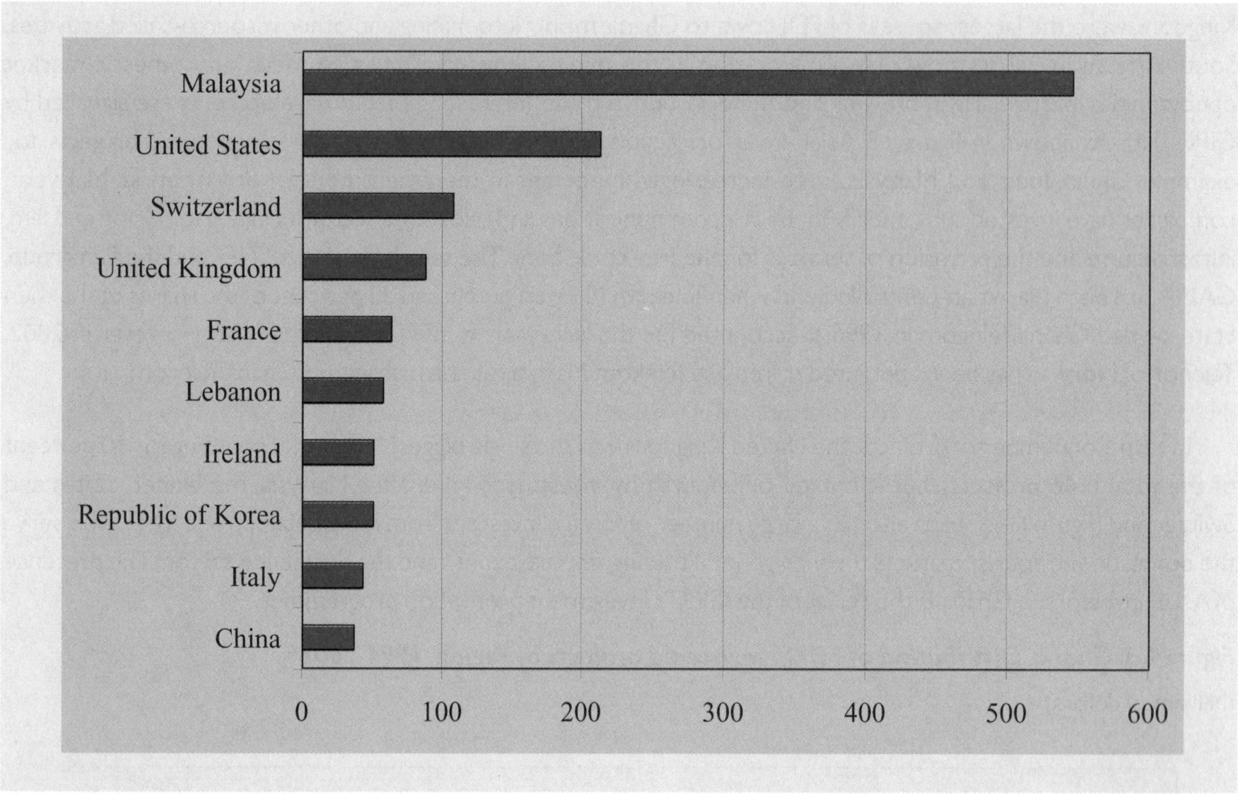

Source: GIPC, Ghana. * FDI in oil and mining are excluded.

B. Impact of FDI

As levels of FDI inflows have not been high in Ghana, their impact is not widely felt except in particular sectors and in select areas such as capital formation, employment generation and transfer of technology and skills.

1. Foreign direct investment and capital formation

External capital inflows have been important for Ghana but the share of FDI in these inflows has been small. There is a considerable gap between savings and investment: in 1980-1999, domestic savings as a proportion of GDP was about 6 per cent compared to an average of 16 per cent for sub-Saharan Africa; while domestic investment as a proportion of GDP was 13.9 per cent, compared to an average of 19.1 per cent for sub-Saharan Africa.[7] The savings-investment gap has been bridged through external capital flows. The contribution of FDI to capital formation in Ghana was low (5 per cent) compared to the average for sub-Saharan Africa in 1996-1999 (figure I.5).

---

[7] World Bank, *African Development Indicators,* 2002, CD-ROM.

Figure I. 5. FDI as a percentage of GFCF in Ghana and sub-Saharan Africa, 1980-2000

(Percentage)

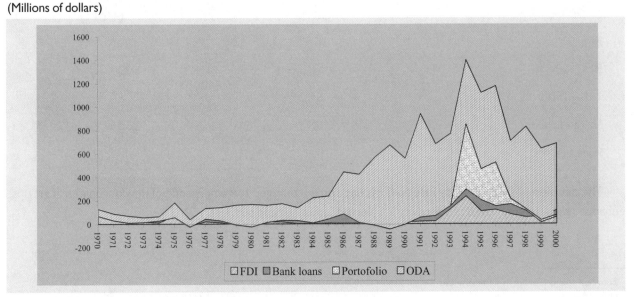

Source: UNCTAD FDI/TNC database.

With the launching of the Economic Reform Programme in 1983, Ghana became a large recipient of official development assistance (ODA) that helped to bridge the domestic savings and foreign exchange gap. ODA inflows in 1990-1999 contributed to more than 50 per cent of capital formation (compared to the sub-Saharan Africa average of 34 per cent)[8].

ODA inflows were linked to some FDI projects, which received the support of aid agencies for long-term loans and grants; they also provided funds for infrastructure development and trade policy facilitation programmes, including customs rehabilitation and the establishment of free trade zones (FTZs). The share of ODA inflows in total net resource inflows declined in 1993-1998 as private flows surged, but the shift was due to a rise in portfolio investment (see figure I.6)

Figure I. 6. Net resource flows into Ghana, 1970-2000

(Millions of dollars)

Source: World Bank (2001). *World Development Indicators.*

[8] Data sourced from World Bank (2001), *World Development Indicators,* CD-ROM.

The rise in portfolio inflows was a complement to FDI in privatization. Much of the large movements of foreign portfolio investment in the Ghana stock exchange (GSE) have been driven by privatization (41 per cent of the stock market capitalization is made by Ashanti). The experience of the GSE – the third largest stock market in Africa – over its 12-year history should be seen as a relatively positive example of capital deepening and widening, despite the fact that in 1999 it suffered a setback, recording the worst performance in the region.

2. FDI, employment and technology

FDI has had direct and multiplier effects on the level of employment, its quality, and the skills of the labour force. But in some sectors it has not contributed to promoting labour-intensive activities. In mining, for example, capital-intensive production has created relatively few low-skilled jobs but it has led to productivity improvements and skills upgrading. Over time, Ashanti has built its own engineering and managerial capabilities and it has programmes for training and enhancement of labour force skills[9].

In other sectors, estimates for the GIPC-registered projects suggest that $1.4 billion of FDI generated jobs for 72,384 Ghanaians and 4,652 non-Ghanaians over 1994-2002. Local employment creation, not particularly high, was mainly in manufacturing, which accounts for 30 per cent of total employment in registered projects.

FDI linkages are also noticeable. An UNCTAD survey of small and medium-sized enterprises (SMEs) with linkages with foreign firms or export activity shows that firm size has increased in the last five years (table 1.3)[10]. Whereas in 1995 only one third of the sampled firms employed more than 20 people each this had increased to almost three quarters of the firms by 2000.

Table I. 3. Employment generation in sample firms with foreign linkages, 1995-2000

(Percentage)

Number of employees	in 1995 or year of establishment	in 2000
1 – 5	30	6
6 – 20	38	26
21 – 50	16	28
51 – 100	4	22
101 – 150	6	8
151 and above	6	10

Source: UNCTAD survey.

The diffusion of technology by foreign firms has also encouraged the emergence of new occupational groups, enhanced skills and improved productivity in selected industries and services.

---

[9] Source: Ashanti Goldfields Company Ltd. *Annual Report,* 2000.
[10] UNCTAD, with the assistance of Empretec Ghana, surveyed 50 firms in Ghana in 2001, having associations with foreign firms. Enterprises included those involved in garment manufacturing, aluminium products, handicrafts and carving, furniture making and agri-culture-related business.

(a) New occupational skills and higher wages

Employment creation in non-traditional exports reflects FDI in key activities, resulting in poverty reduction, particularly for rural households involved in crop production and handicrafts. FDI has also encouraged new occupational skills in information technology that pay high wages, in particular to women (see the section on FDI potential in chapter III).

New specialized occupational skills include producing and marketing organic food (see box I.2). FDI has also played a role in developing the garment industry in Ghana. However, labour productivity and industrial relations have proved difficult in the start-up of garment production, which typically operates under special subcontracting agreements (see chapter II for the case of Volta Garments). Production contracts have been relatively less popular in African countries than, for example, in Asia, and training of labour and labour laws has proved inadequate, so far, to make this kind of production viable in Ghana.

(b) Training

The coverage and technical content of education does not respond to investors' requirements. Managerial skills are an area of concern. TNCs often find that the average Ghanaian university graduate lacks the kind of exposure to the international standards they require; thus on-the-job training is a way of helping redress the skills shortage. The UNCTAD survey found that Ghanaian firms, particularly in the agricultural processing sector, considered training and information about market opportunities to be among the important aspects of the aid provided by foreign firms (see annex II, table AII.1).

In fish canning, for example, a foreign affiliate reported a sharp increase in productivity level after in-house training was introduced. FDI also developed capacity to use new technical equipment – as in the cases of AGRICO and ACS/BPS – or new systems of organization and management, as in Unilever, which established an owner-driver distribution system, (boxes I.2. and I.3). Another common channel for developing new skills and mechanisms is that of TNCs' affiliates, notably international banks, who send their staff for training and experience to other branches worldwide.

(c) Technology

Generally, enterprises in Ghana have low technical capability and low productivity. A survey of five industries – textiles, garments, food processing, woodworking and metalworking – concluded that the general level of technical capacity in Ghana was very low by the standards of not only developed countries but also of industrializing countries in Asia and Latin America.[11]

---

[11] UNCTAD (forthcoming). *Transfer of technology: Case studies.*

Box I. 2. Improving access to technology in agriculture

The Indian-owned family business, Agricultural Engineering Ltd. (AGRICO), has used its experience in India to introduce an intermediate, appropriate technology to Ghanaian rural workers that suits both the physical and economic conditions of the host country. For example, it costs less and allows for easier maintenance. AGRICO has designed and produced a wide range of machinery for agricultural industries in Ghana, Guinea, Nigeria, Liberia, Togo and Upper Volta.

These industries include sugar-processing, coconut-processing (including machinery for manufacturing coir fibre, ropes, doormats and other products) and also construction, for which AGRICO has developed a red-brick alternative to cement.

Technology transfer occurs not only directly through the import of the machinery and equipment itself, but also indirectly, by bringing technical experts and advisers to Ghana, and training domestic workers in engineering and agricultural skills. It has trained more than 300 technicians and engineers, many of whom often have set up their own small-scale industries in local towns. In this way, technical skills and "know-how" can cascade through the domestic economy.

Source: UNCTAD survey.

Notwithstanding the difficult operating conditions, FDI has increased significantly the stock of technology by providing machinery and equipment and it has helped build up local industrial capabilities by contributing to skills formation. This contribution has been strong in the exploitation of natural resources, where the use of capital-intensive technology has developed a pool of trained labour.

Capital-intensive technology used in mining has also resulted in the shifting of surface open-pit operations underground. FDI has also brought technology and marketing knowledge to new export-oriented industries such as agribusiness and downstream processing industries (e.g. wood and fish processing). In agriculture, the transformation of traditional farming geared to local consumers into intensive production for export has involved the adoption of a new set of technologies. Pineapple and organic vegetables are successful examples. Services have benefited from the new information technology, distribution and logistic support of the TNCs (box I.4).

According to firms surveyed by UNCTAD, product improvement, constituted the most relevant support to local firms, followed by training, provision of machinery and equipment together with information on market opportunities (figure I.7).

Figure I. 7. Support to local firms by foreign sources, ranked by importance, 2001

(Percentage of firms citing "important" or "very important" for individual factors)

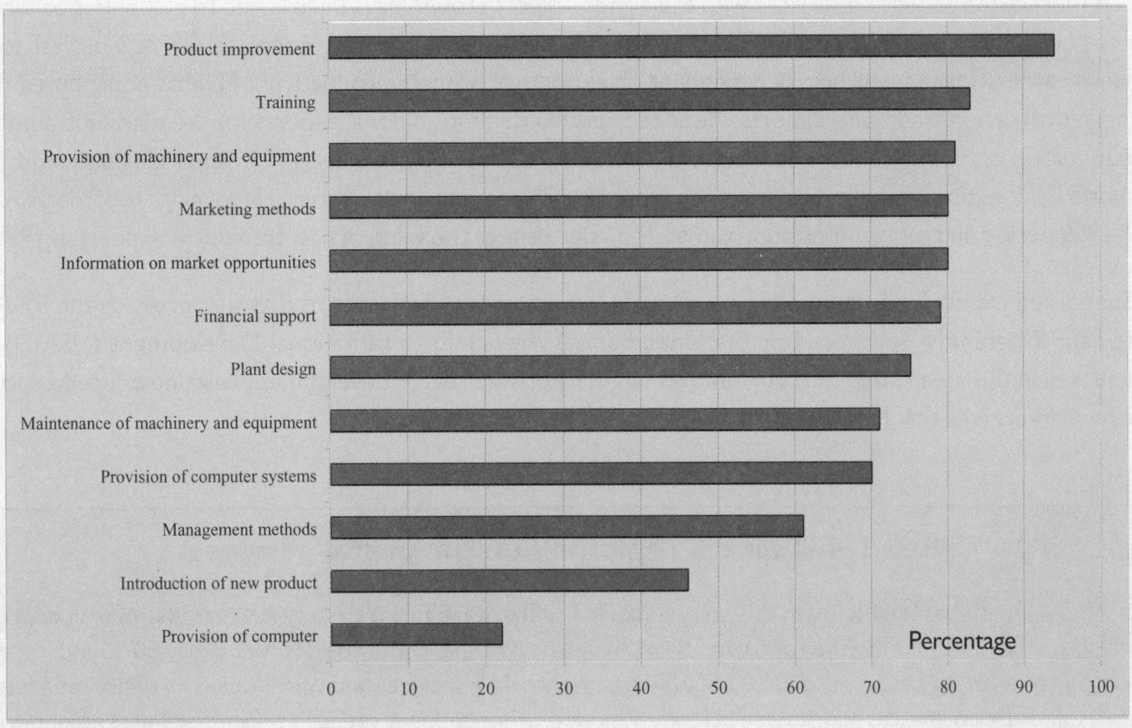

Source: : UNCTAD survey.

Box I. 3. Unilever Ghana Ltd.: creating direct and indirect employment

Unilever has been in what is now Ghana for over 200 years ; it is therefore a unique example of FDI. It also offers an interesting case study in that it combines many of the "classic" ingredients of FDI by a TNC: it owns raw materials, which it processes into manufactured goods that are then packaged, labelled, branded and advertised. Since all the various aspects of production and consumption are featured in this chain, it offers many interesting levels of interaction and linkages with the host economy. Unilever Ghana Ltd. was listed on the Ghana Stock Exchange in 1990 and had a market capitalization of 262.5 billion cedi in August 2002. It is primarily owned by the Unilever parent group (United Kingdom and the Netherlands), but there are around 25 per cent of Ghanaian shareholders. In 1992, there was a merger of UAC of Ghana Limited and Lever Brothers Ghana Ltd. with Unilever Ghana Ltd., and further consolidation is planned for the future when the three companies currently in West Africa (Ghana, Côte d'Ivoire and Nigeria) will merge as a single company chaired from Ghana.

Unilever employs around 1,200 farmers in the two palm oil plantations it owns (a traditional means of ensuring secure supply of primary ingredients) plus another 800 in its processing factory in the Tema industrial area of Accra. However for every one person employed directly by Unilever, it is estimated that another three are employed indirectly through an independent entrepreneurs' distribution network, which distributes Unilever products. Unilever also has a well-developed formal structure for the transfer of human skills and know-how between its direct employees. In 2000, it spent 2.8 billion cedi on local and overseas training. A larger number of regional training courses are planned, and Unilever set up a foundation for education and development and expected to spend around 5 billion cedi on training in 2002. In addition, top managers are regularly sent to work in one of the 75 countries worldwide where Unilever has a presence, thus offering them exposure to different social and work environments with their different ethos, expectations, markets and technologies.

Source: UNCTAD survey.

3. FDI and trade

FDI is important for the development of exports and there are clear linkages between FDI and Ghana's trade pattern. Most of the goods and services with the highest export growth have been linked to FDI. This is particularly true of gold, which, in 2000, became Ghana's single largest export, replacing cocoa as Ghana's biggest foreign exchange earner. Ghana is still heavily dependent on exports of primary products, but FDI has contributed to the recent growth of non-traditional exports.[12] Total receipts from non-traditional exports, for the year 2000 amounted to $626 million or 30 per cent of total exports – a share that has doubled since 1995. According to a study from the World Bank, exports from foreign firms accounted for 75 per cent of the increase in earnings recorded over the 1993-1999 period and represented approximately 34 per cent of the value of non-traditional exports in 1999.

Specialized export funds targeted to develop non-traditional exports, such as that supported by the Trade and Investment Programme sponsored by the United States Agency for International Development (USAID) have worked well in this area. Other aid programmes targeting private sector development have introduced exporters to niche markets (see box 1.5).

Box 1. 4. Accra: a regional hub for postal services

TPG, a Dutch-based TNC, with its two brands, TNT and Royal PTT Post, is a global provider of mail, express and logistics services. It employs approximately 130,000 people in 58 countries, serves over 200 countries, and recorded sales of 9.9 billion euro in 2000. TNT has advanced air services and warehouses linking its European depots and it coordinates worldwide distribution, operating under a special service level agreement with KLM Cargo. TNT Express International began operating in Ghana after a Ghanaian senior manager at TNT in the United Kingdom decided to launch the business there. With growing demand for a reliable depot service in West Africa, improved air connections by KLM cargo and availability of low-cost skilled labour, the Ghanaian affiliate grew fast. In 2001, the Ghana Post Company Limited and TNT Express International Ghana signed a joint venture agreement to establish and operate an International Mail Handling Centre for the West African Region. Under the agreement, an international postal hub and spokes transport system was established at the Kotoka International Airport in Accra. The agreement allows Ghana's capital to become a hub for international exchange of mails and parcels between the subregion and the rest of the world. It also offers the opportunity to negotiate lower air conveyance dues for the links between Europe, the rest of the world and Ghana. TNT is expanding its network, taking advantage of the emerging liberalization of the European postal market. TNT Ghana benefits from such expansion, and it has become a service provider for mail distribution for some European countries. The impact of TNT investment in Ghana is limited in terms of direct employment, since the company only hires about 30 people. However, indirect employment is much larger and spread over various areas. Its technology, export services and cost efficiency are an invaluable contribution to enterprises – foreign and domestic – operating in Ghana. TNT Ghana is confident that if administrative procedures are streamlined, particularly by the customs authorities, it could further expand its business.

Source: UNCTAD survey.

---

[12] Under Ghana's official definition adopted in 1995, non-traditional exports comprise all merchandise exports except cocoa beans, logs and lumber, and mining products.

Table I. 4. Ghana: FDI in selected export categories, 1999

(Millions of dollars and percentage)

Item	FDI exports	Share of total exports
All products	138.80	34
Canned tuna	61.20	99
Cocoa products	40.63	68
Other manufacturers	14.53	18
Processed agriculture products	5.15	16
Agricultural products including fish	7.20	10
Wood products	4.34	5

Source: World Bank (2001). *Ghana International Competitiveness: Opportunities and Challenges Facing Non-traditional Exports.* Report No. 22421-GH.

Exports that have benefited from FDI include furniture manufacturing, which has grown at an average annual rate of 3.5 per cent. At present, it still comprises only half a percentage point of total exports. Other FDI-related exports that have shown growth include canned, chilled and frozen fish products to European markets, and clothing to United States markets. FDI in industries that had initially targeted the domestic market started to export to the West African region. The industries include metal products, cosmetics and plastic products.

Efforts to enhance export-oriented FDI have concentrated on the development of three FTZs under the Gateway Project (see box III.5). Most established firms in the FTZs are in key agro-processing activities which benefit from incentives and preferential market access, mainly to the European Union (EU). By the end of 2000, 32 manufacturing firms were operating under the free zone status. Their total exports amounted to $251 million, accounting for 13 per cent of total exports.

An issue hampering export-oriented investment is that FDI is not spread throughout the country, but is concentrated primarily in the Greater Accra region and the Ashanti region. Within these two dominant regions, however, projects are dispersed and lack the spatial "clusters" and networks often attributed to successful development in other countries. Ghana's FTZs are not defined in geographical or locational zones, but rather relate to the particular characteristics of the firm itself. Thus, one firm in the so-called "free zone" could be located miles away from another firm also qualifying for "zone" status. Similarly a "free zone" firm could be located alongside one that does not qualify for free-zone benefits. This is described in more detail in chapters II and III.

While exports have shown encouraging signs, there are some concerns about imports and the general terms of trade. The rate of growth of imports overtook the rate of growth of exports from the mid-1990s, at 15.8 compared to 13 per cent respectively. Since most imports are for capital and intermediate goods (75 per cent) rather than consumer goods (11 per cent), the implications for future terms of trade are less cause for concern. However, the imported capital stock tends to be of consumable capital goods, such as construction materials, rather than productive capital such as machinery.

Box I. 5. Fair trade: the case of Volta River Estate Limited (VREL)

VREL was established in 1988 to cultivate bananas for export. It combines an interesting mix of commercial and non-commercial principles, where not-for-profit mechanisms have been married to more conventional methods of business. The firm is a Ghanaian-Dutch joint venture with 25 per cent of its shares owned by its workers, and held in trust by Solidaridad, a Dutch non-governmental organization (NGO), which purchased the shares on their behalf. Working conditions are also overseen by the General Agricultural Workers Union, and VREL staff members receive free health and safety care, as well as earning typically 60 per cent above the national minimum salary. VREL has created 720 permanent jobs in an area where income-earning opportunities are seasonal and limited.

The company's 280 hectares of land is strategically located at a number of sites along the Volta River, where the soil conditions are favourable and there is relatively easy access to the port of Tema. However, the firm still experiences many physical barriers to its ability to trade. For example, product quality and sales price are hindered by the lack of pre-cooling facilities at the ports, and the lack of any direct shipping lines from Ghana to the European Union. Agricultural exports from other countries (notably Côte d'Ivoire and Cameroon) arrive in Europe within 10-15 days, whereas it takes 21-25 days for VREL to deliver bananas to Europe. VREL hopes to increase its export base in the near future in order to attract vessels with a direct route to Europe. This will also be beneficial to other non-traditional export sectors that can take advantage of lower freight cost, reduced quality problems caused by transit time and a more reliable supply chain.

In 1996, VREL was certified as a Fair Trade banana producer by May Havelaar Foundation, under the umbrella organization, Fair Trade Labelling Organization (FLO). Once a producer is registered with the FLO banana register, it can sell to a company that has the licence to import and market Fair Trade products. Fair Trade bananas are marketed by Agrofair, a marketing cooperative formed by Fair Trade banana producers and exporters from Ecuador, Ghana and Costa Rica in the 1990s.

VREL needed the support of the Fair Trade framework to find a market, but there are many more benefits that flow from its association: Fair Trade not only guarantees a minimum price to farmers throughout the year, but also ensures the maintenance of high levels of employment, social and environmental practices. For example, VREL is required to maintain herbicide and fertilizer standards that should make its bananas particularly attractive to health and environment-conscious consumers. This may prove more profitable in the long term. In addition, the methods of farming under Fair Trade are more labour-intensive, thereby adding employment in the sector. Finally, Fair Trade funds are used to improve staff living conditions, pay for health and sanitation on the plantations, provide support to nearby communities and invest in environmentally sustainable projects.

VREL is establishing a pilot, 60-hectare organic banana farm that will be converted to organic production in the future. This could help Ghana become a major banana exporter, given growing consumer preferences for organic products. However, a niche market is not a sufficient comparative advantage; Ghana will also have to address the infrastructure constraints facing exporters to fully realize its export potential.

Source: UNCTAD survey.

4. Overall impact

The impact of FDI is best seen in terms of its contribution to growth and improvement of services in key sectors of the economy. These are discussed below.

(a) Mining

In gold mining, FDI has introduced capital-intensive technology, which led to a spectacular increase in gold production, by 500 per cent between 1990 and 2000. Ghana has become the second largest African producer after South Africa. Downstream processing, however, is limited. In the case of aluminium, within the framework of a special agreement for the exploitation of bauxite, local processing has been possible thanks to the investment of Kaiser Corporation (United States), which established Valco. A proportion of Valco's aluminium is retained inside the country for local processing. However, there are regular complaints about input content (i.e. that Kaiser uses alumina from its own mines in Jamaica and elsewhere rather than using Ghanaian bauxite). Valco retains only 10 per cent of its output for domestic industry and there may be scope for negotiating a higher level to encourage even greater expansion in domestic processing capacity (see box III.3 in chapter III).

(b) Infrastructure development

In the Government of Ghana's view, the privatization programme is considered important for infrastructure development. Receipts from privatization have eased the pressure on fiscal accounts, revamped the Ghana Stock Exchange (GSE) and increased foreign investment, with private capital injections enabling the restructuring of former loss-making firms. But other benefits from privatization have not materialized in terms of employment, costs, and improved quality, range and coverage of services.

Given the monopolistic nature and externalities of many infrastructural services, regulatory functions are very important in ensuring that public monopolies are not replaced by private foreign monopolies, without the incentives and pressures to invest and to improve services. This regulatory capacity needs to be strengthened (see chapter II).

FDI has contributed capital, technology and managerial skills for large infrastructure projects (at times co-financing aid projects). For example, the United States TNC, Kaiser Corporation, investing in Ghana's aluminium smelter, Valco, has also been linked with the construction of Tema port and the Akosombo dam managed by the Volta River Authority (see box III.3 in chapter III).

The introduction of foreign capital and expertise into Ghana Telecom helped initiate the transformation of service provision in Ghana: direct exchange lines increased from 78,000 in 1997 to 230,000 at the end of 2001. The number of payphones has increased from only 480 to 4,000, and 10,000 more are planned over the 2002-2005 period. New technologies provided by foreign investors include the introduction of GSM telephones, – which will benefit particularly people living in remote areas where there is no fixed lines coverage – and an integrated services digital network (ISDN) that will facilitate Internet access. Progress in these critical areas for business has already prompted FDI in regional hub activities, including manufacturing, transport and distribution services (box I.4). Prior to privatization, Ghana's telephone penetration (number of telephones per 100 people) was about 0.4, compared to 4.0 for Botswana, 5.1 for Namibia, 0.2 for Uganda, 0.5 for Mozambique and 0.6 for Equatorial Guinea.[13] Telephone penetration should rise to 2.0 by the end of next year. Despite such progress, there is still unsatisfied demand and the quality of service has not improved to the required standards (see chapters II and III). In February 2002, the Government abrogated its management contract with Telekom Malaysia and appointed Telenor of Norway as the manager of Ghana Telecom. Telenor is expected to expand the number of fixed lines from 240,000 to 400,000 within two to three years covering towns that are not connected to the network at present, and to improve service quality and provide more training of staff.

(c) Banking

In Ghana, international banks provide a critical "gap-filling" role, offering the full range of corporate banking services required by foreign investors in handling international transactions. The presence of foreign banks in Ghana also encourages the entry of other foreign companies in ways that go beyond providing international financial services – in terms of advice, information and facilitation – to potential investors. They improve the products and services available to domestic customers by offering a range and quality not otherwise available, and their presence prompted local banks to upgrade their existing facilities. Some of the foreign banks have integrated more deeply with the local economy, with local offices, taking local deposits and employing Ghanaian staff. However, financial laws in Ghana prohibit foreign banks from offering mortgages; while the credit side of the business may be local, lending is primarily with other foreign firms. The trend of foreign firms borrowing domestically means that they have an even greater need of the facilities that an international bank can provide; for example, a foreign firm that finances its investments in cedi needs to be sure that dollar-denominated trade credit is always available. It also has the side effect of tightening the domestic credit market as local enterprises compete alongside foreign ones for capital.

C. Conclusion

The market-friendly Economic Reform Programme (ERP) introduced in 1983 represented the first stepping stone to a revival of private investment in Ghana. A sound investment framework was established, first by opening up the mining sector – with the adoption of the Mining Code in 1986 – and then by the enactment of the Investment Code of 1994. The Code was considered at that time the best in Africa. It eased investment entry and establishment, and provided guarantees and incentives to foreign investors. These measures and the privatization of SOEs, as well as a gold rush put Ghana on the international investors' map as an attractive investment location, generating significant FDI in the first half of the 1990s.

However, in the second half of the decade, FDI declined, both in absolute terms and compared to alternative FDI locations. In recent years, Ghana has had relatively low levels of FDI compared to other developing countries in sub-Saharan Africa and elsewhere, despite the fact that Ghana has regularly been cited as an attractive location for foreign investors.

---

[13] UNCTAD (1998). *World Investment Report 1998: Trends and Determinants*, United Nations publications sales no. E.98. II.D.5: 189.

The drop in FDI means that Ghana has not been able to reap the benefits that a more stable flow of investments could bring, such as providing a buffer for the nation's various foreign exchange requirements, or providing a valuable boost to domestic savings that are low both in absolute terms and compared to the rest of Africa. Domestic savings (as a proportion of GDP) are less than the average for sub-Saharan Africa. Some of the main reasons for the FDI decline include the deep economic crisis generated by external shocks, macroeconomic imbalances and difficult relationships between the Government and management in privatized enterprises. In 2000, FDI flows recovered with early signs of renewed investor confidence in the ongoing stabilization of the economy and in the political resolve of the new Government to promote private sector development, regional integration and good governance.

Despite low levels of inflows, the contribution of FDI to Ghana's development has been important over the years, as evidenced by the size of FDI stock and its impact in sectoral terms. Investment by foreign firms in mining, agribusiness, telecommunications and financial services has helped contribute to employment, exports, foreign exchange receipts, tax receipts and other features of the domestic economy. FDI has played a key role in improving quality and access to services and utilities, and through demonstration effects and dissemination of experience, it has had spin-off effects on other private sector undertakings. Ghana has attracted TNCs from diverse sources in Europe, Asia and North America. Specific targeted promotion initiatives in Asia have been particularly successful. FDI is therefore more significant in the Ghanaian economy than it appears to be when one looks only at the macroeconomic indicators.

The national market in Ghana is not large enough to warrant a huge influx of FDI; the country has therefore pursued access to markets through various bilateral, regional and multilateral trade agreements. The Gateway strategy has targeted export-oriented FDI, which has played a lead role in developing exports of non-traditional products, albeit from low levels. But Ghana has not fully reaped the benefits of export-led growth because of several constraints faced by exporters.

The private sector has had to function in conditions of unstable macroeconomic management, inadequate technology, poor infrastructure and lack of credit facilities. The lack of domestic capital and capabilities has proved to be an indirect but substantial obstacle to attracting FDI in export-oriented manufacturing. Recent efforts to restore greater macroeconomic stability should benefit FDI, but there is also a range of constraints affecting the business sector that need to be tackled. A key objective should be to provide an investment environment that enhances the competitiveness of businesses and of the Ghanaian economy as a whole. A vibrant domestic private sector could also act as a catalyst for attracting FDI. The new Government has acknowledged the challenge and new policy initiatives will be reviewed in the following chapters.

II. The investment framework

Openness to FDI has been a tenet of Government policy for many years. Investors enjoy fundamental rights, guarantees and protection, and benefit from the rule of law enforced by the judiciary and enshrined in Ghana's Constitution. Despite these positive attributes, implementation of some policies could be more effective and could benefit from changes in the regulatory framework and administrative system and structure.

A. Specific FDI measures

1. Entry and establishment

In 1994, Ghana's Parliament enacted and promulgated the Investment Promotion Centre Act to regulate all FDI, except in minerals, oil and gas and the free zones. Sector-specific regulations also apply to FDI in fishing, forestry, and certain services such as banking, insurance and real estate. The Act was aimed at easing the establishment of businesses and attracting investment. It created the Ghana Investment Promotion Centre (GIPC) to deal with all aspects of the FDI regulatory framework, in sectors covered by the Act.

Investors intending to do business in Ghana first have to register as business entities (i.e. limited liability company, partnership or sole proprietorship) with the Registrar-General's Department under the relevant laws.[14] Enterprises with any foreign participation (i.e. wholly foreign-owned enterprises or joint ventures) must then register with GIPC indicating the amount of foreign capital invested. Under the GIPC Act, wholly foreign-owned enterprises must have a paid-up capital equivalent to $50,000.

Where the foreign investor intends to enter into a joint-venture partnership with a Ghanaian, a lesser minimum equity capital of $10,000 is required. Minimum capital requirements are low compared to other developing countries[15]. Foreign investment in trading companies faces more stringent entry requirements. Trading companies, whether wholly or partly foreign-owned, require a minimum foreign equity of $300,000 and the firm must employ at least 10 Ghanaians. The higher minimum investment (required in trading companies) is clearly intended to dissuade foreigners from engaging in this kind of activity. The law, however, recognizes that FDI might be necessary in larger businesses - for example in the retail trade and supermarket chains.

A foreign investor is required to satisfy the minimum equity capital requirements; either in cash transferred through Ghana's banking system, or its equivalent in goods, plant and machinery, vehicles or other tangible assets imported to establish the enterprise. The goodwill of a business - or services rendered by partners - cannot be used to satisfy the minimum foreign equity capital. There is no screening process and registration with GIPC is automatic, although procedures are cumbersome (see box II.1).

---

[14] An entrepreneur, irrespective of nationality, can set up a business enterprise in Ghana in accordance with the provisions of the Companies Code, 1963 (Act 179), the Partnership Act, 1962 (Act 152), or the Business Name Act, 1962 (Act 151).

[15] While Ghana's minimum requirements are rather low compared to other developing countries that impose them (e.g. in the United Republic of Tanzania, it is $300,000 for wholly-owned affiliates and joint ventures), it should be pointed out that most developing countries have abolished such requirements.

Box II. 1. Step-by-step process for establishing an investment project

STEP 1: Registration with Registrar General's Department. Incorporate a company at the Registrar General's Department. The department has five working days to complete formalities if all documents are in order.

STEP 2: Compliance with minimum equity contributions, where applicable. Foreign investors should then comply with the GIPC Act 478 regarding minimum equity requirements. This may be either in cash or in kind. In the case of cash contributions, the investor needs to open a bank account in the name of the company and deposit the cash by a bank transfer or as physical cash. A bank-to-bank transfer of the minimum equity requirement has to be confirmed to the Bank of Ghana by the investor's local authorized dealer bank.

The Bank of Ghana, in turn, confirms this transaction to GIPC for the company's registration purposes. Physical cash carried into Ghana by individuals for investment purposes should be declared on the requisite Bank of Ghana Form on arrival and subsequently deposited in a bank account within the shortest possible time. The transaction should be confirmed by the investor's dealer bank and the Bank of Ghana similarly to a bank transfer. In the case of equity in kind in the form of imported machinery, equipment and goods, all documents covering such imports should be in the name of the registered company and should be submitted to GIPC.

These documents include a bill of lading/airway bill; destination inspection certificate; customs bill of entry; import declaration form; certified/final invoices; and evidence of capitalization form. Destination inspection certificates are issued by one of two inspection organizations: Gateways Services Ltd or GSBV (or some other similar inspection organization approved by the Ministry of Trade and Industry), stating the value and condition of the goods. [16]

STEP 3: Concessionary duty items. Zero-rated and equipment concessionary duty items should be cleared automatically and directly through CEPS. Essential plant, machinery and equipment, which fall under Section 24 of the GIPC Act should be cleared with the GIPC.

STEP 4: Registration with GIPC. Foreign investors then register with the GIPC, which has five statutory working days to complete the registration process, provided the registration forms are in order.

STEP 5: Immigrant Quota. All wholly Ghanaian-owned enterprises and enterprises with foreign participation seeking immigration quota facilities in respect of expatriate personnel (experts) for their businesses should satisfy the relevant minimum capital requirements (Section 30 of Act 478).

STEP 6: Registration with IRS and VAT Secretariat. All enterprises must register directly with the Internal Revenue Service (IRS) and the Value Added Tax (VAT) Secretariat for purposes of determining the statutory tax (e.g. taxes, rebates, and exemptions thereof).

STEP 7: Environmental Impact Assessment Certificate. Enterprises must register and obtain an environmental permit from the Environmental Protection Agency (EPA).

Source: UNCTAD survey.

---

[16] The cost of the destination inspection is the equivalent of 1 per cent of the value of the goods being imported.

Outside the act, limitations on the right of establishment apply as follows:

♦ **Restrictions by sectors**

In fishing, non-Ghanaians may own a maximum of 50 per cent of the interest in a tuna-fishing vessel. A limit of 40 per cent foreign ownership also applies to insurance companies. In the mineral and oil sectors, the State has the right to a 10 per cent share at no cost.

♦ **Restrictions on the stock exchange**

Foreign ownership of a publicly-listed company on the stock exchange cannot exceed 75 per cent.

♦ **Privatization**

The transfer of public enterprises to the private sector has been an important element of the economic programme since 1983. The divestiture process is open to foreign investors. No ownership requirements are imposed, however preference is given for local participation of at least 25 per cent.

The following aspects of the regulatory framework warrant reforms:

♦ **Ownership requirements**

There are not many limitations on foreign ownership. However, if Ghana wishes to attract further FDI, the limitations could be reviewed.

♦ **Registration**

There are several government departments involved in registration. The Act provides for time limits within which they should complete their formalities. However, the time limits prescribed are subjected to the rather vague condition that the department must be satisfied that "all relevant documents for registration are in order".[17] Legal provisions on the appraisal and procedures for registration need to be simplified.

2. Treatment and protection of FDI

Ghana's Investment Act does not make any specific reference to standards of treatment. Although the track record of investor treatment in Ghana has been non-discriminatory, investment treaties could provide additional guarantees of treatment standards.[18] Ghana has entered into bilateral investment treaties (BITs) with a number of capital-exporting countries. Most of these agreements were signed and ratified between 1989 and 1992 and a number of others have been signed but are still awaiting ratification, (table II.1).

Ghana's network of BITs remains fairly small, and efforts should be made to expand it. In addition to the BITs, some treaties for the avoidance of double taxation have also been entered into and others are under negotiation (table II.2).

---

[17] Compare, for example, the criterion for the appraisal of minimum equity requirements that is clear under section 19(2).
[18] UNCTAD (1998). *Bilateral Investment Treaties in the mid-1990s*, United Nations publication sales no. E.98.II.D.8.

Table II. 1. Bilateral investment promotion and protection agreements with Ghana

Other parties to the agreement with Ghana	Status	Date of signature	Date of ratification	Date of entry into force	Duration (years)
United Kingdom	Signed and ratified	March 22, 1989	March 26, 1991	October 25, 1991	10-expired
Netherlands	Signed and ratified	March 31, 1989	March 26, 1991	January 1, 1991	15
China	Signed and ratified	October 12, 1989	March 26, 1991		10
Switzerland	Signed and ratified	October 18, 1991	June 26, 1994	June 16, 1993	10
Denmark	Signed and ratified	January 13, 1992	October 28, 1998	January 6, 1995	10
Germany	Signed and ratified	February 24, 1995	October 28, 1998		10
Bulgaria	Signed	March 31, 1989			10
Egypt	Signed	September 14, 1989			10
Romania	Signed	September 14, 1989			10
Malaysia	Signed	November 8, 1996			10
Côte d'Ivoire	Signed	November 4, 1997			10
South Africa	Signed	February 26, 1999			10
Italy	Signed	July 9, 1998			10
United States (OPIC)	Signed	February 26, 1999			10
France	Signed	March 26, 1999			10
Benin	Signed	May 18, 2001			10
Burkina Faso	Signed	May 18, 2001			10
Mauritius	Signed	May 18, 2001			10
Mauritania	Signed	May 18, 2001			10
Guinea	Signed	May 18, 2001			10
Zambia	Signed	May 18, 2001			10

Source: Ghana Investment Promotion Centre, 2001.

Table II. 2. Double taxation treaties with Ghana

Parties to the agreement	Status	Date of signature	Date of ratification	Date of entry into force	Duration (years)
United Kingdom	Signed	January 20, 1993	Not yet ratified		
France	Signed	April 5, 1993	Not yet ratified		
Italy	Under negotiation		Not yet ratified		

Source: Ghana Investment Promotion Centre, 2001.

Ghana also has a model BIT, now used as a basis for negotiations, which has provisions covering the three key areas of standards of treatment (box II.2)[19]. Such model clauses facilitate negotiations, and in the past five years, the number of BITs signed has doubled. However, there are still a number of treaties waiting for ratification.

Box II. 2. Ghana's model bilateral investment treaty provisions on treatment standards

ARTICLE 3
Protection of Investments

(1) Investments of nationals and companies of each Contracting Party shall at all times be accorded equitable treatment and shall enjoy full and adequate protection and security in the territory of the other Contracting Party.

(2) Neither Contracting Party shall, in any way, impair by unreasonable or discriminatory measures, the management, maintenance, use, enjoyment or disposal of investments in its territory of nationals or companies of the other Contracting Party.

(3) Each Contracting Party shall observe any obligation it may have entered into with regard to investments of nationals or companies of the other Contracting Party.

ARTICLE 4
National Treatment and Most-Favoured-Nation Provisions

i.   Neither Contracting Party shall in its territory subject investments or returns of nationals or companies of the other Contracting Party to treatment less favourable than that which it accords to investments or returns of its own nationals or companies or to investments or returns of nationals or companies of any third state.

ii.   Neither Contracting Party shall in its territory subject nationals or companies of the other Contracting Party, as regards their management, maintenance, use, enjoyment or disposal of their investments, to treatment less favourable than that which is accorded to its own nationals or companies or to nationals or companies of any third State.

Source: Ministry of Foreign Affairs, Ghana, 2001..

(a) Protection against expropriation

Ghana's Constitution prohibits the compulsory taking of private property without compensation. The GIPC Act reflects this, guaranteeing that a foreign-owned enterprise shall not be subject to expropriation or nationalization unless appropriation of it is in the national interest and for a public purpose (section 28 of the GIPC Act).

In case of expropriation, compensation is overseen under the Act on the basis of a "fair and adequate" valuation of the property. The Act also provides that compensation shall be paid in convertible currency and without undue delay. This is in line with the trend in recent BITs with the increasing usage of what is commonly referred to as the "Hull Formula", which calls for prompt, adequate and effective compensation.[20] The GIPC Act provides that the value is to be determined by the High Court of Ghana.

---

[19] See UNCTAD (1996). *International Investment Instruments: A Compendium*, United Nations publications sales no.E. II.96.A.11
[20] The formula, named after former United States Secretary of State Cordell Hull, who was one of its strongest proponents, sets the standard of compensation, which is supported by the major capital-exporting countries.

(b) Dispute settlement and arbitration

Ghana's legal system is based on Common Law supplemented by specific legislation. Judicial independence is enshrined in the Constitution and all investors – foreign and domestic – have equal access to the courts of law. Investment- or business- related disputes can be settled through the normal process of instituting civil suits. In addition, alternative dispute settlement mechanisms, such as arbitration, mediation and conciliation, are also being increasingly encouraged by the Government, not only within the judicial system but also by NGOs which promote private-sector-led dispute settlement processes.[21] The Arbitration Act of 1961 (Act 38) provides the legal basis for regulating the settlement of differences by arbitration, and the enforcement of arbitration awards in Ghana. The Arbitration Act also makes provision for the enforcement of foreign awards in accordance with the United Nations Convention on the Recognition and Enforcement of Foreign Arbitral Awards, adopted in New York on 10 June 1958.

Section 29 of the GIPC Act provides that any dispute between an investor and the Government which is not amicably settled, may be submitted to international arbitration under one of three methods of third-party dispute settlement. These are: arbitration in accordance with the rules set by the United Nations Commission on International Trade Law (UNCITRAL); or within the framework of an international agreement on investment protection; or pursuant to any other international machinery for the settlement of investment disputes (Ghana is also a member of the International Centre for Settlement of Investment Disputes (ICSID) and of the Multilateral Investment Guarantee Agency (MIGA).

If the parties cannot reach agreement on any of the three methods, the choice of the investor shall prevail. The GIPC Act guarantees the right to international arbitration not only for foreign investors, but all investors covered by the Act (i.e. including those local investors registered with the GIPC). Guaranteeing nationals the right to international arbitration (at their choice) is uncommon.

Ghana's respect for foreign investors' legal concerns over dispute settlements and conflict resolutions contributes to improving the policy environment in the country. However, to ensure consistency, the Arbitration Act of 1961 needs to be reviewed so as to be in line with the principles enunciated in the GIPC Act of 1994.

(c) Transfer of funds guarantees

Ghana has no restrictions on the conversion and transfer of funds. The country's foreign exchange regime was gradually liberalized over a period of years following the inception of the structural adjustment programme in 1983. By 1990, the exchange rate was market-determined. Today, Ghanaian cedis are easily exchanged for dollars and most major European currencies.

There is growing use of inter-bank and private foreign exchange bureaux. With specific reference to foreign investors, it is also important to note that section 27 of the GIPC Act guarantees the unconditional transferability (through any authorized dealer bank in freely convertible currency) of dividends, interest payments, technology-transfer fees and the remittance of the proceeds of sale by an enterprise.

---

[21] The Ghana Arbitration Centre established in 1996, and the Commercial Conciliation Centre established in 1998.

Ghana's foreign currency needs are met largely through gold and cocoa export revenues and donor assistance. The fall in world prices of these commodities since 1999 led to temporary foreign currency shortages, which caused delays in the acquisition of foreign exchange and constrained the transfer of funds even in the absence of official restrictions. These difficulties have since subsided and the Government has asserted its commitment to achieving balance-of-payments objectives without intervention in the exchange market or the introduction of quantitative controls.

B. Conditions of operation

1. Taxation

In the new Tax Law (Act 592, 2000), corporate tax rates have been reduced from 35 per cent to 30 per cent for companies listed on the Ghana Stock Exchange, and to 32.5 per cent for unlisted companies. However, foreign investors consider the corporate income tax as being high.[22] The rate of the withholding tax has been increased from 5 per cent to 7.5 per cent. Furthermore, as part of its means of raising funds after the 1999 economic crisis, the Government established a levy, known as the National Reconstruction Levy, to be sourced from banks, pension funds and insurance companies during the period 2000-2002. Another levy of 2.5 per cent of the gross profit before tax of companies operating in Ghana was imposed from 2000 to 2002. Businesses also must pay value added taxes (VAT) and other indirect taxes such as customs duties. Two aspects regarding the income tax system are of concern to both foreign and domestic investors:

♦ **Fiscal stability**

Unforeseen changes in the fiscal burden – which occurred in the past two years – affect business planning and undermine investors' confidence.

♦ **Tax administration**

Income tax remittance regulations have an adverse effect on the working capital available to firms. It is noteworthy that in Ghana, the Government assesses a firm's tax liability at the start of the year and payments are made on that basis. The problem is that many firms are eventually audited after extensive delays of up to as much as four years. Some firms have had to hire additional staff for months just to assemble the required documentation for reconciliation. Many firms report that their refunds are much lower than what they applied for-since the tax authorities had archived many of the original files necessary to compute the right amounts. The Government needs to consider revising the audit procedures and applying international standards.

2. Investment incentives

Ghana provides a variety of incentives for foreign investors. These include tax holidays, capital allowances, locational incentives, customs duty exemptions and other inducements. These are specified in the relevant statutes and applied fairly. Relevant legislation includes the following:

---

[22] Corporate tax rates are similar to those applied in other African countries – Botswana: 25 per cent, Côte d'Ivoire: 25-35 per cent, Senegal: 35 per cent and South Africa: 30 per cent. It is interesting to note, however, that a lower corporate tax, of 15 per cent, is applied in outward-oriented economies such as Hong Kong (China), the Republic of Korea, Taiwan Province of China, Chile and Mauritius.

- Income Tax Decree, 1975 (as amended);
- Free Zones Act, 1995, Art. 504;
- Income Tax (Amendment) Act, 1998, Art. 551; and
- Ghana Investment Promotion Centre Act of 1994.

Many of Ghana's incentives are of general application. However, a number of them have a narrower focus, and some apply to specific regions (box II.3).

Box II. 3. Investment incentives, benefits and guarantees

Tax incentives provided under the Income Tax Decree, 1975 (as amended) include:

1. Tax holiday (from start of operations)

a) Real estate: Rental income from residential and commercial premises for the first 5 years after construction. Income accruing to a company engaged in the construction, sale or letting of residential premises during the first 5 years of start-up of operations.

b) Rural banks: 10 years.

c) Agriculture and agro-industry: Cocoa farmers and cocoa producers: income exempted; cattle ranching: 10 years; tree crops (e.g. coffee, oil palm, shea butter, rubber and coconut): 5 years.

d) Air and sea transport (non-resident): Income exempted. The President may exempt any persons or class of persons from all or any provision of the Act subject to the approval of Parliament.

e) Value addition to local raw materials: Manufacturing enterprises that use local raw materials enjoy a 3-year tax holiday.

2. Capital allowances (vary by sector): Accelerated depreciation on machinery and equipment – 5 per cent for all sectors of the economy except banking, finance, insurance, mining and petroleum; and 20 per cent for building and real estate services.

3. Locational incentives (tax rebate): Manufacturing industries located in regional capitals other than Accra and Tema will enjoy a 25 per cent rebate. All other manufacturing industries located outside regional capitals shall enjoy a 50 per cent rebate.

4. Corporate tax rate: The tax rate in all sectors is 32.5 per cent except for income from non-traditional exports (8 per cent) and hotels (25 per cent.

5. Exemption from income tax: An exemption will apply for the provision of accommodation for employees on farms, as well as building, timber, mining and construction sites.

6. Loss carry-over: All sectors are allowed five years.

Source: GIPC, 2001.

For example, tax rebates are granted to manufacturing companies located outside Accra, Tema, and other regional capitals. Locating banks in rural areas is another priority: the rate of tax on banks that locate in rural areas is only 8 per cent (after their 10-year period of tax exemption).

Other incentives are by sectors: special incentives are granted to enterprises engaged in agriculture, hotels, manufacturing, construction and other activities detailed in the Ghana Investment Code and the Income Tax Act. For example, whereas the corporate income tax rate is 32.5 per cent, companies in the hotel industry are taxed at 25 per cent. The building industry also receives incentives. The income accruing to a company engaged in the construction for sale or rental of residential premises during the first five years following the commencement of operations of the company is exempt from tax. The rental income from any residential or commercial premises is also exempt from tax for the first five years following completion.

Incentives focus on promoting exports. Exporters receive additional incentives, such as retention of foreign exchange earnings from manufacturing and agricultural products, and up-front duty exemptions and duty drawbacks (see box II.4).

Box II. 4. Special incentives available to exporters

◆ **Export retention:** Under this procedure, exporters of non-traditional items are permitted to retain 35 per cent of their export earnings in a foreign account with the Ghana Commercial Bank in London for the importation of inputs for their operations and for payment of related services such as foreign business travel expenses, participation in trade fairs, medical and educational bills as well as wages for expatriate staff.

Such holdings may also, at the request of an exporter, be converted to local currency for the exporter's domestic use. Exporters of traditional items are allowed to retain 20 per cent, except exporters of round logs and Ashanti Goldfields products, who retain 50 per cent and 45 per cent, respectively.

◆ **Duty drawbacks:** Manufacturers are entitled to 100 per cent of the import duty and other taxes on imported raw materials if such raw materials are used for export production.

◆ **Income tax rebate:** Companies or individuals who engage in exports are entitled to tax rebates ranging from 60 to 70 per cent, depending on the percentage of total output exported.

◆ **Bonded warehousing:** Exporters are allowed to store their raw materials in warehouses under the control of the Customs, Excise and Preventive Services (CEPS) without payment of import duty and other taxes until the goods are withdrawn from the warehouse.

◆ **Export duties:** Exporters of non-traditional items are exempted from paying duty on exports. Exports of gold, bauxite, manganese and timber are, however, subject to a 6 per cent export tax. The tax on cocoa is the difference between export proceeds and payments to farmers together with operational costs, if the proceeds exceed payments.

Source: Ghana Free Zones Board (GFZB), 2001.

Particular attention is paid to companies engaged in non-traditional exports.[23] Such exporters are taxed at a reduced rate of 8 per cent and are exempted from some export duties. Ghana also has a number of FTZs that provide further incentives to exporters. The zones consist of areas in which infrastructure services – including bond warehouses and utilities such as power, water and telecommunications – are provided to export-oriented businesses. Goods traded between FTZs and other countries are exempt from customs duties. There are extensive incentives for companies setting up in the FTZs, including:[24]

♦ Zero per cent income tax for 10 years and a guarantee that income tax thereafter shall not exceed 8 per cent.

♦ Total exemptions from payment of withholding tax from dividends arising out of investments in FTZs.

♦ Relief from double taxation for foreign investors and employees.

♦ No import licensing requirements.

♦ 100 per cent foreign ownership allowed.

♦ No restrictions on repatriation of profits.

The Free Zones Act also allows firms that export 70 per cent of their production to obtain "free zones status" even if established outside the zone. According to the UNCTAD survey, investors receiving free-zone benefits are satisfied with the incentives offered, particularly for fast track clearing of imports (see box II.5). Combined with other income tax rebates for exporters, the incentives are very generous compared to other countries in the region. However, granting free zone status to companies located outside the zone has created problems for the zones' development. They continue to lack adequate infrastructure facilities, and this is impeding the clustering of activities originally sought.

Box II. 5. How attractive are Ghana's Free Zones?

According to an investor - Carnaud Metal Box, a French TNC based in Tema, the benefits of being licensed as a Free Zone Enterprise are as follows:

♦ The creation of a one-stop regulatory authority – Ghana Free Zones Board (GFZB) – reduces the time-consuming process of dealing with multiple agencies, and problem-solving is eased;

♦ Free Zone Enterprises obtain postponement of otherwise up-front payment of duties on raw material imports;

♦ These enterprises are entitled to fast-track clearance for imported inputs from various ports of entry;

♦ Trade transactions with customers is made much more responsive to customers' needs since there is more flexibility in the supply system;

♦ The 10-year tax holiday encourages business expansion;

♦ GFZB provides support in dealing with labour issues, particularly immigration;

♦ Free zone status helps reduce production costs, making possible competitive sales prices;

♦ Free Zone Enterprises have leverage in the business community and with government institutions.

Source: Ghana Free Zones Board (GFZB), 2001.

---

[23] Non-traditional exports are those other than cocoa, coffee beans, timber and logs, electricity, and unprocessed gold or any other mineral in its natural state.

[24] To qualify, firms must export 70 per cent of production.

How attractive are incentives to potential investors? According to the UNCTAD survey, incentives offered, other than the free-zone benefits, are still inadequate. Investors have pointed out the need for improvement in areas such as technology, education, access to credit and fiscal incentives. Among firms interviewed, the foreign affiliates were most dissatisfied with incentives relating to technology and education (67 per cent) (see annex II, figure AII.4). The focus on export incentives seems to have stifled attention to the importance of technology upgrading and human resource development.

Besides incentive schemes that are outlined in detail in the law and are of general application, Ghana also allows for certain incentives to be contractually negotiated with specific investors. In this connection, sections 25 and 26 of the GIPC Act are particularly relevant. Section 25 provides that for purposes of promoting strategic or major investments, the GIPC Board may, after consultation with other State agencies and with the President's approval, negotiate specific incentives with investors. In addition, section 26 provides that the Board may specify priority areas of investment for which special incentives and benefits would be applicable.

The rationale for these discretionary incentives is unclear. The following can be considered for upgrading the incentives to FDI:

♦ Enlarge the scope of incentives to take into account technology upgrading and human resources development.

♦ Make more transparent the evaluation criteria for the granting of additional incentives by the GIPC Board by issuing regulations or guidelines to be made available to all potential investors.

3. Labour

Labour regulations and policies in Ghana are generally favourable to business. Law sets a minimum wage but it is low,[25] and many foreign firms pay well above the minimum wage. Ghana's labour regulations and practices are in some cases restrictive compared with practices applied internationally in countries hosting similar investments.

For example, Ghana's labour force is not familiar with firm-level productivity-based pay schemes, which are not covered by the legislation currently in force. The case of a foreign-owned garments exporter, Volta Garments, which had to close due to its inability to meet contract terms and negotiate a pay scheme, is instructive (box. II. 6).

Some aspects of the labour legislation are in need of review. The cost of severance pay is in most cases higher than international norms.[26] This adds up as extra costs to investors, and can stifle the development of labour-intensive export production. Moreover, labour-rights provisions are generally negotiated under firm-specific collective bargaining agreements that can involve a lengthy and difficult process. Recently, some strikes have resulted in closure of businesses, such Volta Garments mentioned above. In other cases, labour unions competing for influence in the workplace have caused serious disruptions.

---

[25] At current exchange rates, it is less than $0.50 a day.
[26] For comparison with other developing countries, see International Labour Office (2000). *Termination of Employment Digest*, Geneva, ILO.

Box II. 6. Volta Garments: a lost opportunity?

Volta Garments, set up in 1992 by foreign investors from Hong Kong with the aim of exporting shirts to the United States, was the first large garment exporter established in Ghana after the trade reforms of the late 1980s. In the first few years of operation, as the firm tried to develop its workforce and establish its reliability in world markets, it paid workers basic monthly salaries along with a bonus scheme based on fulfilling production targets.

As basic worker skills began to improve and quality approached acceptable levels, Volta tried to institute a standard piece-rate pay scheme. Such schemes are used in many countries to provide incentives for greater productivity. The unions and Volta's workers rebelled against the proposed piece-rate pay scheme principally on the basis that it had not been "formally introduced in the labour laws of Ghana". In the end, Volta could not negotiate an acceptable pay scheme. The firm, already facing other difficulties in meeting its contract terms with regard to delivery and quality, was finally forced to close down, resulting in the loss of 300 jobs.

Source: UNCTAD survey.

These isolated events have tainted the reputation of Ghana's workers, undeservedly, since labour relations generally have been peaceful. However, such episodes show the need to revise the provisions of the labour laws to improve conflict resolution, for example by introducing improved mechanisms for dealing with strikes. Current labour laws do not require arbitration and cooling-off periods. Employers and workers involved in firm-level collective bargaining should have access to appropriate training in areas such as labour relations, negotiation and conflict resolution.

While foreign investors may be attracted by Ghana's large pool of inexpensive, unskilled labour, they continue, however, to depend on expatriate management. Ghana facilitates this by not imposing discriminatory or excessively onerous visa requirements. In fact, an investor who invests under the GIPC Act of 1994 is entitled to an automatic immigration quota.

The number of people who benefit from this quota depends on the size of the investment: an investment of $10,000, or its equivalent, made in convertible currency or machinery and equipment, entitles an enterprise to one automatic immigrant quota; an investment of $10,000 to $100,000 entitles an enterprise to two automatic immigrant quotas; and Section 30 of the law provides that an investment of $500,000 and above gives an enterprise four automatic immigrant quotas. An application for even more extra expatriates can be made, but it is then incumbent on the investor to justify why a foreigner must be employed rather than a Ghanaian. There are no restrictions on issuing of work and residence permits to free zone investors and employees.

Since Ghana wishes to improve labour competitiveness, policy adjustments may be necessary. A new labour bill has been drafted to amend and consolidate the laws relating to labour, employers, trade unions and industrial relations. It also envisages the establishment of a National Labour Commission to provide for consultation and settlement of conflicts related to labour issues.

4. Performance requirements

Ghana does not uphold performance requirements for establishing, maintaining or expanding a business, though certain requirements have been tied to the privatization programme. For example, in telecommunications, companies have to meet performance targets, failing which their licenses are revoked. Ghana has no local-content arrangements.

5. Import and export regime

The Imports and Exports Act of 1995 governs Ghana's import-export regime. There are no specific requirements for exporters of non-traditional goods. Export permits are required for wildlife, timber products, precious minerals, fresh fish and antiques. The export of logs is banned. Listed "traditional" items such as raw coffee beans, sheanuts, gold bullion, uncut and unpolished diamonds, manganese ore and bauxite, are exported by State-owned export organizations such as the Ghana Cocoa Board (COCOBOD) and the Precious Minerals and Marketing Corporation.

However, government guidelines released in July 2000, allowed for partial liberalization of cocoa exports by introducing quotas to allow licensed buying firms to export a maximum of 30 per cent of their cocoa bean purchases. Foreign currency surrender requirements apply to cocoa and gold exporters. For each export transaction, they must provide bank-approved exchange- control forms.

Ninety-eight per cent of export receipts from cocoa beans must be surrendered, with a retention allowed of 2 per cent. For gold, the retention is set by agreement between the Government and the companies; on average about 25-30 per cent is surrendered. Exporters of non-traditional goods can hold up to 100 per cent of export receipts in offshore foreign currency accounts to buy imported inputs and meet other permitted business expenses.

The 1995 Act also governs the importation of goods into Ghana for commercial purposes. Generally speaking, investors do not face any restrictions on importation of inputs.[27] While Ghana's import-export policies are mostly well conceived, their implementation often falls short of what is intended and has, at times, even worsened the situation.

Under the Gateway Project, the Customs, Excise and Preventive Services, (CEPS) are working towards improving customs efficiency (see chapter III, for a description of the Gateway Project). However, two particular problems have retarded these efforts. The first arises out of the project's own improvement efforts.

As part of these, CEPS introduced destination inspection and transaction-based valuation of consignments, and reorganized the way documents are processed. But while all these changes were meant to generate improvements, the transition to the new destination inspection and valuation scheme, together with the CEPS reforms, increased delays in an already long clearance process. The escalated delay charges and interest accrued on import taxes have meant increased costs of imported inputs for exporters. The second problem relates to delays in paying duty drawback and VAT refunds on imported inputs. While the system for VAT credits works better, some exporters have experienced greater difficulty in receiving duty drawbacks.

---

[27] However, certain imports require special permits. For instance, permits for pharmaceutical products are issued by the Ministry of Health; and arms, ammunition and explosives by the Ministry of Interior.

Without a prompt, well-functioning duty drawback system exporting is not attractive, and as long as this persists, foreign investors will shy away from Ghana.

In addition, the Commissioner of CEPS also has legislative authority to grant concessionary rates, usually zero, on inputs for specified end-uses imported by approved manufacturers.[28] These arrangements undermine the transparency of the tariff structure and can be a major source of malfunctioning in the customs administration. Some concessions, coupled with VAT exemptions granted to beneficiaries of the Commissioner's concession, even put domestic producers or potential producers of such inputs (for example bicycles) at a disadvantage. Improvements can be made with regard to import and export measures directly affecting FDI, as follows:

- **Tax credits**
  The lack of a functioning drawback system undermines the ability of exporters to compete. If adequate budgetary provisions for duty drawbacks cannot be made, tax credits should be introduced.

- **Inspection and valuation scheme**
  The Government should: (i) rigorously enforce the performance standards for the inspection of companies and rapidly reduce valuation times; and (ii) provide adequate information to investors and exporters about any new procedures.

- **Tariff policy**
  Remove inconsistency in the tariff structure and strengthen the effectiveness of the CEPS.

6. Access to land

There are three categories of land ownership provided for in the 1992 Constitution of Ghana, namely:

(a) public lands (i.e. State land and land vested in the President in trust for the people of Ghana);

(b) stool lands (community lands vested in traditional/other community leaders on behalf of the community); and

(c) private and family/clan lands (owned by families, individuals and clans in the community). Foreigners are prohibited from owning land, but can lease it – through negotiations with the Government, the local chief, or the relevant private individual(s).

Furthermore, while Ghanaians can have leaseholds for up to 99 years with a possibility of renewal, foreigners, on the other hand, are not allowed, by law, to take leases of land (whether for residential, commercial, industrial or agricultural purposes) for more than 50 years. This is probably not much of a disincentive for most foreign investors as even those interested in long-term projects are likely to be satisfied with a period of at least 50 years. But foreign investors face other serious legal as well as bureaucratic obstacles in the area of land access.

---

[28] Under Chapter 98 A of the Customs tariff on "Goods Admissible at Concessionary rates When Imported by Manufacturers Approved by the Commissioner". Eligible goods include materials used in the manufacture of agricultural implements and machinery, machetes, fishing nets, pharmaceuticals, plastic pipes and tubes, mosquito nets and coils, bicycles, iron rods, corrugated building sheets and nails.

First, foreign investors find it difficult to deal with the extensive network of government agencies, traditional chiefs and individuals involved in obtaining land. Difficulties include unclear and long negotiation processes, sometimes with several parties at different stages of the process, and thus often ending with insecure tenure arrangements. For example, in the case of stool land, at times the legality of the deal may be called into question if the understanding between the parties at the time of purchase is not implemented immediately and the chief happens to die or is overthrown and the new chief brings up new terms and conditions.

Secondly, the land available to foreign investors is itself very limited. Industrial-zone land is particularly scarce. Of course, the Government could acquire land compulsorily for investors if the acquisition could be argued as being in the public interest. The Constitution of Ghana makes provision for the acquisition of land by the Government through the Compulsory Acquisition Law, and the State Lands Act and Stool Lands Act provide guidelines for implementing such acquisition of land from stools, families and individuals. But the question is: When does public interest arise, and could that be said to include acquiring land to give to a private investor?

Thirdly, even where the prime land for a specific project is identified, there is the problem of finding the true owners of the particular lands. Often, the land is subject to litigation and the issue of clear title over land remains a big problem in Ghana. There is also a problem of boundaries identification. All this means that a thorough search at the Lands Department to ascertain the identity of the true owner of land offered for sale is extremely important. But in some cases, land records are incomplete or non-existent, and therefore clear title may be impossible to establish.

Fourthly, once title is established, processing documents with the Lands Commission and Land Title Registry is often delayed. A period of up to 3–6 months is typical for completing the process of obtaining land, but delays can reach one or two years.

Land policy is restricting FDI, particularly investment in the development of agribusiness, and a variety of initiatives are needed to address existing bottlenecks. The following reforms could be considered:

♦ **Promote land banks and support investors**

The Ghana Investment Promotion Centre (GIPC) has established a Land Bank with information on land and real estate available on lease, rental or equity for investment purposes. The Government should help establish additional comprehensive Land Banks. It should be noted that GIPC does not offer much help to a foreign company to get through the process of acquiring land. It responds to requests and gives investors information on required formalities, but does not guide investors through the maze of regulations and deal-making required to acquire the land. The GIPC should take a more proactive role in supporting foreign investors in this area. A land acquisition support desk dedicated specifically for that purpose should be established at GIPC and should have a direct link to the Lands Department.

♦ **Strengthening the commercial justice system**

Specialized land courts could be established to ease congestion in the current commercial justice system; alternative dispute resolution should also be encouraged in that regard.

C. Other policy issues

I. Technology and protection of intellectual property

Ghana is a member of the World Intellectual Property Organization (WIPO) and a founding member of the African Regional Industrial Property Organization. Ghana joined the Paris Convention in 1976 and is a signatory to the Patent Co-operation Treaty of February 1997. The country is also a member of the Universal Copyright Convention and a signatory to the Agreement on Trade-Related Aspects of Intellectual Property Rights (TRIPs).

While recognizing the importance of technology, Ghana remains mired in traditional thinking on how to regulate the entry and acquisition of foreign technology. Under the GIPC Act, a technology transfer agreement must be registered with the Investment Promotion Centre to be legally effective (Section 22 (2)). This requirement is outdated and needs to be removed. Section 33 (3) of the Act also provides that all technology transfer agreements shall be governed by any regulations that are applicable at the time when such agreements are concluded. Such regulations may place conditions with respect to financial and temporal terms of transfer. Ghana's legislation should clearly define and regulate the terms of such contractual arrangements.

On one hand, there may be a need to prohibit restrictive covenants in the agreements that are anti-competitive. As Ghana is also in the process of conforming its legislation to the TRIPs agreement, it should be noted that article 40 of the TRIPs agreement makes clear that member States remain free to adopt measures to prevent or control restrictive clauses in the agreement that restrain competition. Among such measures are those assisting local companies to obtain information on various and competing sources of technology. Thus, as long as measures taken under section 33 (3) of the GIPC Act conform to the requirements of the TRIPs agreement, they should not present difficulties.

On the other hand, it is critical that the Government regulations do not expand into the realm of contractual terms of business transactions. Best practices in this area point towards a policy of protection of intellectual property rights, coupled with a legal and information base that ensures these rights maintain and support a competitive and nurturing environment for businesses.

Patent protection exists under the Patent Law of 1992. It provides for a patent protection term of 10 years with two renewable periods of five years. In order to comply with TRIPs, legislation needs to be amended to extend protection coverage to 20 years. Other areas earmarked for improvement to comply with WTO TRIPs agreement are geographical indicators and industrial design.

The Registrar-General's Department has the responsibility for registering patents, trademarks and industrial designs. The Patent Law authorizes the Registrar-General to register patents locally, as well as those granted under international protocols to which Ghana is a signatory. Patents filed in Ghana are verified with other patenting authorities and granted - if found patentable. With regard to copyrights, a new copyright law to replace the 1985 Copyright Act has been approved by the Government and is soon to be passed into law. The Copyright Office administers copyright protection.

A monitoring team, comprising officials from the Copyright Office and members of the Ghanaian Copyright Society, monitors compliance of copyright legislation. Its functions are to be expanded under the new copyright law. Copyright disputes are settled by arbitration, with the Copyright Administrator acting as arbitrator. If unsuccessful, legislation also enables copyright holders to invoke court action to protect their intellectual property, and to seek damages and seizure of offending material. Copyright infringement is also a criminal offence subject to imprisonment and/or fines. Penalties are to be increased substantially under the new legislation, including imprisonment of up to five years.

According to WIPO, the Trade Marks Act of 1965 has several shortcomings relating to service marks, treatment of well-known marks, and exclusive rights to registered marks. Criminal procedures also do not provide adequate protection against counterfeiting of trademarks. A new Trademark Amendment Bill has been submitted to Parliament with a view to legislative amendments to comply with the requirements of the TRIPs Agreement.

The music industry provides a successful example of copyright protection. Ghana implemented the "Banderole" system of identifying genuine musical works in 1992 to control pirated products. Only those carrying this adhesive authentication label can be sold legally in Ghana. According to officials, this system has successfully controlled piracy of musical works; piracy rates have fallen from 90 per cent to about 10 per cent for local works and 25 per cent for foreign works. The new legislation will also protect computer software in a similar manner.

2. Competition

Ghana does not have in place legislation on competition. A draft bill is currently undergoing legislative procedures. The objective is to provide fair competition and consumer protection by establishing an independent regulatory authority. The Government is conscious of the importance of a well-enforced competition law to protect consumers from uncompetitive practices. This issue is particularly relevant for the privatizations of public monopolies, in which private investors, including foreigners, are encouraged to invest.

3. Environment

Although Ghana has the policies, laws and institutions needed to adequately protect its environment, extreme water pollution and growing deforestation and soil degradation indicate the need for further action - according to a comprehensive review of environmental management in Ghana carried out by the Ministry of Environment.[29]

The report recommends updating environmental legislation enacted in 1994 and strengthening the coordination role of the Environmental Protection Agency to facilitate environmental impact assessment. The report also highlights the need for the development of a more efficient energy production system and for protecting forests from extensive logging for fuel wood.

---

[29] World Resources Institute, www.wri.org and Environment Information System: www.eis-africa.org.

D. Special regimes

I. Mining

The revision of policy and legislation relating to mining was a specific and integral part of Ghana's Economic Recovery Programme initiated in 1983. New legislation was promulgated in 1986: the Mining and Minerals Law (PNDC Law 153). This law introduced a number of reforms, including financial incentives, new State institutions and the major rehabilitation of State-owned mines. Under the legislation, all minerals are owned by the State. Exclusive mining rights are granted by the Ministry of Mines and Energy following well-defined parameters specified by the Law.

The legislation applies equally to Ghanaians and foreigners, except for the provisions relating to artisanal mining and exploitation of construction minerals that are reserved for Ghanaians. However, the Ghanaian Government is entitled to a free carried equity interest of 10 per cent of mineral ventures. It also has the option of purchasing an additional 20 per cent at a fair market price. The law prescribes the maximum periods for reconnaissance, prospecting or mining leases as well as the maximum acreage that can be authorized per licence for prospecting or mining (table II. 3).

The law is flexible enough to leave certain matters (especially those relating to the fiscal regime) open for negotiation between the investor and the State. Negotiable matters include deferment of royalty payments, work programmes, and the level of the export earnings retention allowance.

As for the regulation aspects, an investor in Ghana's mining sector has to deal with a number of government institutions. These include the Ministry of Mines and Energy, (responsible for the mining industry); the Geological Survey Department (responsible for geological studies including map production and maintenance of geological records); and the Mines Department (responsible for health and safety inspections and maintenance of mining records).

Table II. 3. Types of mining rights under the Mining and Minerals Law

Licence type	Reconnaissance	Prospecting	Mining lease	Restricted lease
Purpose	Regional exploration, not incl. drilling	Search for minerals and valuation	Extraction of minerals	Building and industrial minerals
Area	No limitation on size	150 km²	50 km² per lease up to maximum of 150 km² per company	
Period	12 months, renewable	2 years, renewable, with reduction of area to not less than half	30 years, renewable	

Source: Minerals Commission of Ghana

Also relevant are the Lands Commission, which keeps legal records of licences and has responsibility for the legal examination of new applications; and the Environmental Protection Agency that has overall responsibility for environmental issues related to mining.

Apart from government institutions, another important organization is the Minerals Commission – essentially a mining industry members' club. Apart from being extremely influential in its recommendations on mineral policy, it is also often the first contact for prospective investors and an important source of essential information for them.

Since the 1986 revisions and new legislation, few additional reforms or mineral policy reviews have been carried out. To some degree, this may reflect the success of the 1986 reforms in balancing the need for adequate regulation of the mining industry with the provision of adjustable fiscal incentives for investors. But today Ghana's fiscal regime for mining is not competitive compared with some other countries (see table II.4). In particular, the following aspects should be noted:

♦ Investors' after-tax returns are low

While Ghana's fiscal regime is well structured - in that high early capital allowances permit reasonably prompt investment pay-back - the high fiscal take increases the risk to the investor that the after-tax return will be unacceptably low.

Under the fiscal regime for Ghana's mining sector, tax deductions are possible with a depreciation allowance of 75 per cent of the capital expenditure incurred in the first year of investment and 50 per cent of the declining balance in subsequent years; and there is an investment allowance of 5 per cent in the first year only.

Table II. 4. Comparison of mining fiscal regimes in selected countries

(Percentage)

Item	Botswana	Ghana	United Rep. of Tanzania	Peru	South Africa
Royalty	3-5	3-12[a]	3-5	0	0
Witholding tax on dividends [b]	15	3.5	10	0	12.5
Witholding tax interest on loan	15	5	None	None	20
Witholding tax on salaries and fees of foreign consultants	15	5	3	None	None
VAT on capital goods for mining	None	None	None	None	None
Depreciation allowance	..	75[c]	100	20	12.5[d]
Government equity requirement	15	10	None	None	None

Source: UNCTAD survey.

a   All minerals.
b   Remitted abroad.
c   In the first year of production, 50 subsequently, using the declining balance method.
d   Compound.

Furthermore, losses in each financial year not exceeding the value of the capital allowance for the year may be carried forward and there is an allowance for capitalization of all pre-production expenses approved by the authorities when the investor starts development of commercial mining. With regard to the fiscal take, the Government is entitled to acquire a free carried equity interest of 10 per cent in any mining venture and has the option to acquire an additional 20 per cent participatory interest at a fair market price.

In addition to this, the holder of a mining lease is required to pay royalties that can vary between 3 per cent and 12 per cent of the total revenue of the minerals obtained from the mining operations. The variation is related to the "operating margin" and is designed to prevent royalties becoming too onerous during times of low profitability. A mining leaseholder is also required to pay annual rental charges as prescribed by regulations. Furthermore, the holder of a mining lease is required to pay income tax at the rate of 32.5 per cent and an additional profit tax of 25 per cent as provided under the Additional Profit Tax Law 1985 (PNDCL 122). All these add up to a very high fiscal take for the Government.

◆ Ghana's fiscal regime is less attractive for investment than that of competitor countries

A recent financial modelling of Ghana's regime - in comparison with that of five leading or rapidly emerging mining countries - shows its fiscal take to be highest and the most onerous on the investor in Ghana.[30] Fiscal "take" is measured as net present value of State take from taxes, royalty and concessional State equity where applicable. For the mining projects modelled, Ghana's long-term fiscal take from gold mining was twice as high as that of the United Republic of Tanzania, which is the most investor-friendly fiscal regime of the sample.

It should be noted that these results assume that no export duty is applied to minerals, and the main conclusion is therefore likely be even stronger if it assumes that export duty is applied in practice. Whilst Ghana's regime is thoughtfully structured so as to aid marginal projects, promote early investment recovery and apply a progressive fiscal take, it needs to be reconsidered in the light of recent moves by competitors to offer more attractive regimes to investors.

Recognizing the need to revise the Mining Law, the Government of Ghana has engaged in consultation with the industry in the drafting of a new law aimed at making the country more competitive vis-à-vis other regimes such as that adopted by the United Republic of Tanzania. The following provisions could be reconsidered when revising the law:

◆ Review relatively high rates of mineral royalty;

◆ Reconsider the right of the State to own 10 per cent equity;

◆ Improve restricted loss carry-forward provision for exploration;

◆ Reduce the relatively high fiscal take;

◆ Allow for fiscal stability agreements relating to licence terms, including the mining development programme or stabilize the fiscal and foreign exchange regime; and

◆ Encourage downstream processing.

---

[30] *Source:* Transborder Advisory Services, a private consulting firm with special expertise on mining policy issues, which has been involved in drafting the New Mining Code in the United Republic of Tanzania. Countries included in the analysis were Chile, Indonesia, Peru, Papua New Guinea and the United Republic of Tanzania.

2.   Fisheries

The Fisheries Law, which is overseen by the Fisheries Monitoring Control, Surveillance and Enforcement Unit of the Ministry of Agriculture, regulates all fisheries activities. The law stipulates that no less than 50 per cent of interest in all tuna fishing vessels must be owned by Ghanaian citizens, the Ghanaian Government, a public corporation, or a Ghanaian limited liability company registered under the Companies Code of 1963 (Act 179).

It also provides that no less than 10 per cent of all Skipjack, Yellowfin, Bigeye and Albacore tuna catches landed in Ghana shall be offered for sale to persons engaged in industrial processing of fish in Ghana. Restrictions on ownership in fishing have affected the industry's ability to raise capital for renewal of fleet and productivity improvements.

The cost of producing and exporting fish in Ghana is higher than elsewhere. Thus Ghana's competitiveness in fish exports is in a shaky position, and depends heavily on EU trade preferences. Under the Cotonou Agreement, Ghanaian exports enter the EU duty-free, while Asian competitors pay GSP duties equal to 24 per cent. This duty differential is quite important because of the unfavourable cost differential.

3.   Forestry

Forestry is the third most important export for Ghana in terms of volume, but the Government is seeking to balance the need for foreign exchange with the desire to protect the environment and the sustainability of the industry. Thus Ghana's stated forestry policy is to promote the sustainable management of forest resources and encourage downstream-processing to create jobs.

Under a new Forest and Wildlife Policy introduced in 1994, the Government initiated a series of control measures, including a ban on the export of logs, designation of reserve areas, and the concept of an "annual allowable cut." The Timber Resource Management Act was also passed to improve the allocation system of logging permits, and, in 1998, regulations were introduced to control illegal chainsaw operators.

The Act also provided for a more efficient and transparent allocation process based on a new contract scheme called Timber Utilization Contracts (TUCs) to replace the ad hoc system being practiced at the time. Under the new system, firms bid for contracts to log particular sections of the forest. Foreign investors are generally satisfied that the duration of these contracts enables them to get a reasonable rate of return on their investment. Each contract has a duration of 40 years, and is renewable as long as the contractor manages its designated logging area according to specified criteria.

However, implementation of the new scheme still suffers from continued malpractice in the vetting and allocation process. For example, some of the allocated contracts are reported to have been given to firms that do not have the capacity to use the timber resources efficiently, and, in some cases, these improperly allocated contracts have been traded to other enterprises for profit, which is contrary to the intention of the scheme. In other cases, the same contract has been allocated to more than one party, resulting in disputes over land title and ownership.

Thus, despite a good forest policy, ineffective policy implementation has meant that Ghana remains in danger of misusing its forest resources. Ineffective policy implementation has also hampered FDI in downstream processing. Thus Ghana's wood industry continues to export products with low value-added. Moreover, there is also the danger of reducing foreign investment interest even further if Ghana is cut out of important export markets because of unsustainable forestry management. Major wholesalers and retailers in the EU already require that the wood products they buy come from "certified" forests. Certification requires evidence that forest utilization is planned for sustainability and enforced effectively to protect both timber and wildlife. Efforts to deal with these issues need to focus on three areas.

- **Auction systems**

  The Government should introduce an auction system to award contracts to the most efficient users. Efforts should be made to attract internationally reputable foreign investors in this business. If properly implemented, the TUC system under the new Act would be an efficient way to manage the country's forest reserves.

- **Certification**

  The Government should promote the "certification" of forest resources to ensure entry into the EU export market and any other markets that have similar standards.

- **Technical assistance**

  The Government should encourage foreign investor partnerships that make available assistance to raise the technical capability of processors at all stages in the value chain, beginning with loggers and sawmillers.

4.   Infrastructure

The Government of Ghana wishes to encourage private participation in the expansion and maintenance of the nation's infrastructure in most subsectors. This is seen as a means of introducing greater efficiency in the infrastructure sector as well as reducing financial constraints on investment. The main regulatory issues are as follows:

(a) Telecommunications

The Ghanaian telecommunications market has long been monopolized by one State-owned corporation. In 1996, the sector was opened up to competition and the national company, Ghana Telecoms, was privatized (with a 30 per cent share bought by Telekom Malaysia) and five mobile phone companies were licensed. While a number of service providers are entering the market, the regulation of telecommunications in Ghana has lagged behind, leaving the door open for anti-competitive practices by operators. In 2002, Telenor of Norway has been appointed for three years as the manager of Ghana Telecom to replace Telekom Malaysia. A new business plan sets out targets including:

- 400,000 new fixed lines by the end of 2005;
- Adequate cellular coverage in all regional and district capitals;
- Internet connection in all Senior Secondary School an Teacher training institutes within three years;
- High-speed data transmission capacity servicing the demand both from public and private sources.

To meet the objectives of the business plan, a capital expenditure of close to $500 million is required. The investments will be funded by vendor-financing, financing from financial institutions, new equity and by the operating cash flow generated by Ghana Telecom. The Government is also taking measures to strengthen the National Communications Authority and promote competitive behaviour.

Foreign investors can play an important role in contributing to the success of privatization, both in generating cash from the sale of underlying services and in injecting new investments to improve them. However, maximizing the benefits from foreign participation in telecoms and ensuring that foreign firms will be interested, requires that three issues, in particular, be addressed:

Unbundling and sequencing. Plans for liberalization in Ghana often have not been accompanied by an appropriate division between production and distribution nor has such a split been appropriately sequenced. In many cases, this has prevented any potential benefit from competition, with no consequent improvement in service or consumer costs.

For example, Ghana Telecom's retention of access to local loop cables has allowed the continuation of monopolistic behaviour and undermined the viability of other operators. Commercial interconnection agreements need to be negotiated with all parties - wire line or wireless operators and State-owned or private companies - receiving fair treatment. All operators should be allowed to carry and terminate international traffic, establishing a level-playing field.

Targeting. In place of competitive pressures – and at least partly because of the weaknesses outlined above – the Government has tended to rely too much on pre-negotiated performance targets that are at times neither feasible nor enforceable. A review of these arrangements by an independent board with appropriate technical capability should accompany broader changes in the implementation of the reform process.

Regulatory capacity. Delays in appointments at the National Communication Authority, as well as understaffing, lack of resources and low institutional capacity to fulfill its mandate, have proved to be a significant barrier to the reform of telecommunications policy.

(b) Energy

Ghana continues to rely heavily on hydroelectricity for its power needs.[31] The State-owned Volta River Authority (VRA) was created to own and manage both the dam and the national grid. A number of regulatory and privatization initiatives are under way to enhance private sector participation in both electricity and oil/gas projects. The Public Utilities Regulatory Commission, established by an Act to set tariffs, has attempted to level the playing field regarding utility costs. The Government is considering to privatize electricity distribution and to bring in private thermal power generators.

---

[31] The main source is the Volta Dam into which the Volta River feeds; its hydroelectric scheme supplies almost all of Ghana's electricity.

With regards to oil, the Ghana National Petroleum Company (GNPC) is the parastatal primarily responsible for the importation of crude and petroleum products. It also has a broad mandate to undertake the exploration, development, production and disposal of petroleum and national gas in Ghana. The Government is currently restructuring GNPC, which, when completed, will focus its activities solely on the exploration of Ghana's hydrocarbon resources. Government policy objectives focus on the deregulation of downstream petroleum supply operations, and divestitures aimed at bringing in strategic investors.

From a policy perspective, there remain two crucial unresolved issues:

* **The unbundling of the national grid from VRA**
  The success of most independent power projects (IPPs) will depend upon the producer securing access to the grid for transmission. Since VRA would be a competitor to the IPPs for energy supply, potential investors are understandably concerned that it may seek to block or otherwise obstruct access to transmission lines. VRA continues to control access by its competitors to the existing lines, thus depriving the sector of the competitiveness that was intended to result from the entry of private firms.

* **Long-term contracts**
  As VRA had done with Valco for Akosombo, many IPPs will seek to have a large anchor customer. Although there are a few industrial customers in Ghana large enough to serve as an individual catalyst for an IPP, such as Ashanti Goldfields which requires more than 100 MW per year, the main customer for most projects is likely to be the State-owned Electricity Company of Ghana (ECG). ECG is slated for eventual privatization, but the sale has been delayed several times. Uncertainty over its ownership, combined with mounting debts and shortages of foreign exchange, have prevented ECG from fulfilling some of its existing contractual obligations and from signing new contracts. A clarification of ECG's future, with guarantees from the Government, would enable some potential projects to move ahead.

(c) Transportation network: shipping, air links and roads

In 1995, the Government published the Free Zone Act that also encouraged the development of commercial and services activities at seaports and airports. In 1996, the Minister of Trade and Industry declared the seaports of Tema and Takoradi, and Kotoka International Airport to be free zone areas. In line with government policy, the Ghana Ports and Harbour Authority aims to invite private sector participation in the activities of the ports, but it has not taken any action on this so far.

With regard to road transportation, most projects are dependent on aid financing and there is no comprehensive framework to encourage private sector financing using tools such as management contracts. There are also attempts to encourage donors away from the financing of individual projects – which had created critical gaps in the network coverage – towards the financing of programmes in partnership with the Government, civil society and the private sector.

E. The role of institutions

The institutional framework for investment is composed of different governmental agencies, and a number of private sector institutions. The key to success of the investment process is to ensure that it is clear and transparent and that there are operating links amongst the institutions involved.

With regard to policy-making, in Ghana the Presidency plays a fundamental role. The Ghana Investment Promotion Centre established in 1994 to administer the Ghana Investment Promotion Act is under the Office of the Presidency. To boost private sector development, the President has recently established, under the Presidency, a Ministry for private sector development. He has also created two task forces on key issues related to FDI. The first deals with privatization and the second with implementing the United States African Growth and Opportunity Act (AGOA). The President encourages dialogue with the private sector, and engaged in a series of meetings with all stakeholders in key sectors (e.g. mining, oil and energy) before planning reforms. In addition, an Economic Forum was held in June 2001 to launch joint public-private sector initiatives to boost growth.

The Government of Ghana also established in 2001, with the assistance of the World Bank Group and the International Monetary Fund (IMF), a small, high-level Investors' Advisory Council, which comprises about 15-20 business leaders, both local and international. The Council will meet twice a year to discuss concrete steps that could be taken to improve the attractiveness of Ghana as an investment location. Council members also agreed to act as Ambassadors to promote Ghana as an investment destination and to support visits of the President abroad, encouraging him to travel with private businesspeople on his future trips.

The key ministries involved in the investment policy area are the Ministry of Economic Planning and Regional Integration, the Ministry of Trade and Industry and the Ministry of Manpower Development and Employment, as well the different Ministries of the key economic sectors such as agriculture, tourism, mining and energy. The new Ministry for Private Sector Development should play a coordinating role in all initiatives regarding investment with a view to reducing bottlenecks. However it is mainly a liaison office, with few resources and limited capacity to assume a leadership role.

The GIPC is responsible for the promotion of FDI and is also primary coordinator for all investments in Ghana.[32] It is mainly responsible for:

♦ Initiating and supporting measures to enhance Ghana's pro-business climate;

♦ Stimulating increased local and foreign investment;

♦ Providing information about business opportunities and sources of investment capital, and advise on the availability, choice or suitability of partners in joint-venture projects;

♦ Identifying attractive investment opportunities and inviting interested investors to participate;

---

[32] However, at the same time, investments in certain sectors such as mining and petroleum exploration are regulated by other specialized agencies.

- Organizing promotional activities to stimulate investment and business ventures;

- Serving as a one-stop liaison between business investors and government departments and agencies, institutional lenders and other authorities; and

- Providing support services to business investors, including assistance for obtaining the necessary permits.

While the GIPC is supposedly the main coordinator of all investments in Ghana, the Government has actually divided responsibility for regulating investment in five main agencies: the Ghana National Petroleum Corporation and the Minerals Commission for investments in the petroleum and mining sectors, respectively; the Divestiture Implementation Committee for investments through the privatization programme; the Ghana Free Zones Board (GFZB), which is concerned with investments in export processing zones; and the Ghana Investment Promotion Centre, which deals with all other investments. While there is a clearer division of labour between the other agencies and GIPC, the roles of the GFZB and GIPC overlap in terms of seeking to attract export-oriented investors. Generally speaking, the multiplicity of agencies in itself does lead to some confusion among investors.

Besides registering FDI, GIPC should act as a "one-stop centre" being mandated to "act as liaison between the enterprise and relevant government departments, agencies and other public authorities" (section 31 of the GIPC Act). This function is not well defined, thus hampering GIPC performance. The role of GIPC in FDI promotion is not well articulated; it needs a focused strategy that targets its investment promotion and makes it a service provider to investors. If GIPC is to become a one-stop shop, all core activities and institutions will need to be linked to it. In particular, it should coordinate all initiatives geared to promoting export-oriented FDI.

F. Overall assessment

Guaranteeing a steady flow of FDI depends critically on a supportive policy and regulatory environment. The 1994 GIPC Act provides investors in Ghana with fundamental rights, guarantees and protection. Ghana offers a favourable rule of law environment, and the independence of the judiciary is enshrined in the country's Constitution. The Government has made progress in improving policies of relevance to investors' decisions. It has announced a comprehensive plan to develop Ghana's potential to become the regional hub for West Africa. However, many policies have not been effectively implemented, partly because of the lack of adequate changes in the regulatory framework and in the administrative system and structure.

Of most relevance to FDI in Ghana is the framework related to mining, forestry, and infrastructure services. As discussed above, many aspects of the mining regime are less attractive for investment than in competitor countries. The Government should introduce an adequate regulatory framework for utilities, and promote the establishment of public-private partnership in infrastructure development. Regulatory authorities should be established or strengthened to regulate and monitor the provision of public services. These authorities should set a code of practice for the utilities. Finally, to further exploit opportunities to attract export-oriented FDI, Ghana needs to remove supply bottlenecks and build specialized trade infrastructure and services to attract FDI.

The bottlenecks facing investors' operations include those relating to company incorporation, labour laws, access to land, and the tax regime and administration. A simple, unified and automatic system for investment registration and company incorporation should be put in place. The FDI entry process should be streamlined, and GIPC should act as a "one-stop" agency for investors, with greater authority and ability to liase with different ministries and institutions involved in the investment process. Access to land, which is critical to investors, should be facilitated by speeding up the process of land clearance and by promoting private development of industrial estates. The GIPC should take a more proactive role in supporting foreign investors in this area. A "land acquisition support desk", dedicated solely for that purpose, should be established at GIPC and it should have a direct link to the Lands Department. Administrative efficiency in tax auditing and improvements in the fiscal regime are needed. Labour laws should be more supportive of flexible working time, and schemes to facilitate firm-level productivity-based pay should be introduced along with mechanisms to ease labour conflict resolution.

Investment policy and procedure reforms require corresponding institutional reforms. To this end, GIPC should be reconfigured and empowered to coordinate all aspects of a well articulated, export-oriented, investment promotion strategy.

III. STRATEGY FOR FDI

Ghana has the potential to be a location of choice for investment and trade in the West African regional market. The Gateway strategy, launched as part of Vision 2020, is basically sound - even though other countries in the region have since emerged as strong competitors. The strategy should be revived and implemented with vigour.

Ghana has so far attracted FDI mainly in natural resources. There is also potential to attract greater investment in non-traditional sectors such as resource-based agro-processed and agricultural products, and in light manufacturing for local and regional markets[33]. Attracting FDI in these areas will require deliberate efforts to overcome key supply constraints: weak infrastructure; low productivity; and a lack of local business partners. More proactive investment promotion efforts are required if Ghana is to regain the front-runner status it had in the early 1990s. In the immediate future, with the economy still in the process of recovery, the main focus should be to encourage existing investors to expand and reinvest. They, in turn, will stimulate new foreign investors to enter Ghana.

A. FDI Potential

1. Ghana's comparative position

Ghana is considered an attractive investment location, according to surveys of business opinion, which regularly rank Ghana high among African countries: Ghana ranked ninth on the 2000 African Competitiveness Index[34], and fourth on an "optimism index", where survey respondents estimate future economic growth (table III.1). The 2001 African Competitiveness Index reinforced this picture, giving Ghana high points for its tax incentives and for allowing repatriation of capital and profits. Political stability and the predictability and reliability of government policies are also lauded.

Table III. 1. West African comparisons: national competitiveness, 2001*

Overall rankings	Ghana	Nigeria	Côte d'Ivoire	Senegal
African Competitiveness Index (2001)	9	20	15	8
Improvement Index[a] (1996-1999)	13	4	14	9
Optimism Index[b] (1999-2001)	5	1	22	17

Source: World Economic Forum, 2001.

*Note: Ranking of 24 African countries, where 1 is best.

[a] Measures perceived changes over the previous three years.

[b] Rates the level of optimism over reforms and improvements.

---

[33] Ghana's official definition of non-traditional exports, adopted in 1995, includes all merchandise exports except for cocoa beans, logs and lumber, and mining products.

[34] World Economic Forum (2001). *The Africa Competitiveness Report 2000/2001*, and 1998/1999.

Within the region, Ghana is more or less competitive with its neighbour, Senegal. Senegal is considered to have better port facilities and marginally quicker customs clearance; however its air transport facilities are rated lower than Ghana's. Senegal has a more educated labour force, but less available skilled labour. It takes less time in Ghana to process permits and licences. Most importantly, Ghana is perceived to have a more reliable legal system, with contracts more likely to be enforced by its courts.

Although Nigeria has the largest market in West Africa, its business environment is perceived to be relatively difficult (in terms of the legal system, civil service and crime). Business would prefer to locate in Ghana and trade with the regional market. Ghana has a higher ratio of trade to GDP than its neighbours, Nigeria and Senegal (table III.2). This partly reflects high import dependence and limited domestic supply capacity. Ghana also has a comparatively high purchasing power in terms of GDP per head. Overall, Ghana is acknowledged to be one of the most attractive and comfortable African countries in which to do business, and live.

Table III. 2. West African countries: comparison of selected economic indicators, 2000

	Ghana	Senegal	Nigeria
Population (millions)	19.3	9.5	126.9
Labour force	9.2	4.3	50.3
GDP (dollars)	5 190.3	4 371.1	41 084.6
GDP growth	3.7	5.6	3.8
GDP (PPP dollars)*	37 913.0	14 386.0	113 662.0
GDP per head (dollars)	413.0	609.0	253.6
GDP per head (PPP dollars)*	1 964.0	1 510.0	896.0
Structure of economy (%):			
Agriculture/GDP	35.3	18.2	29.5
Industry/GDP	25.4	26.9	46
Services/GDP	39.3	54.9	24.5
Trade (%):			
Exports of goods and services/GDP	49.2	35.0	52.3
Imports of goods and services/GDP	69.6	34.8	41
High-tech exports (as % of manufactured exports, 1999)	8	5	27

Source: World Bank (2002). *World Development Indicators.*

   PPP = purchasing power parity.

To sum up, Ghana's main comparative weaknesses relate to its limited market, inadequate infrastructure, and the poor supply capacity of domestic firms, along with certain policy factors: mainly customs, taxation, health and education.

2. FDI potential at the country level

Ghana has a number of strengths and weaknesses important to investors (see table III.3). The strengths include abundant natural resources (particularly minerals such as gold and diamonds); abundant and fertile land; and a climate well suited to agriculture. It is politically stable, and has a reasonably skilled, low-cost labour force. Ghana also benefits from being a member of the Economic Community of West African States (ECOWAS) which comprises more than 200 million people.

Ghana has increased its exports to this regional market, and has experienced an influx of foreign investors who seek access to this larger market and prefer to be domiciled in Ghana rather than in any of the other ECOWAS member States. Ghana is considered an efficient, peaceful and desirable place in which to invest, work and live, compared to other African locations.

The weaknesses, as perceived by existing investors, include: macroeconomic instability; the high cost (and low quality) of utilities – particularly electricity and telecommunications; – and a weak technological base (table III.3).[35] Standards of quality control are seen as generally inadequate and there is a shortage of critical skills - particularly managerial talent. Many of the weaknesses can be overcome.

Ghana has the key strengths to realize its Gateway strategy outlined in Vision 2020 - which seeks to make the country a hub location for trade and investment, and to expand its access to regional markets. This regional trade objective is supported by a number of trade agreements undertaken within the framework of ECOWAS, which envisages West African economic integration. International trade objectives are also supported by a number of trade agreements, the most significant of which are the United States African Growth and Opportunity Act (AGOA), which offers eight years of privileged access to United States garments markets; and the Cotonou Agreement between the African, Caribbean and Pacific (ACP) group of States and the EU – the ACP-EU partnership agreement – that offers preferential entry to EU markets (see box III.1).

The next section outlines FDI potential by sector, highlighting export-oriented opportunities. The final section sets the policy directions to establish an environment supportive of enterprise development and to make FDI an integral component of the Gateway strategy.

3. Potential by sectors

One of Ghana's key strengths is its natural-resource base. This is especially true for its gold mineral deposits, so that mining plays a central role in attracting FDI. However, non-traditional exports (such as agro-processing, services and tourism) have grown rapidly in recent years, and provide new business opportunities to foreign as well as domestic investors.

(a) Agro-processing

Agriculture and agro-processing are among Ghana's key sectors, showing large increases in export revenues (table III.4) and accounting for more than one third of GDP. This growth has occurred despite the fact that commercial production of food and cash crops is still undeveloped, which suggests the potential that exists for further foreign investment aimed at both regional and international markets.

---

[35] A recent survey by the Private Enterprise Foundation reported low utilization of installed capacity due to competition from cheap imports, non-availability of raw material, inadequate working capital, and a fall in demand.

Table III. 3. FDI potential in Ghana: strengths and weaknesses

Strengths	Weaknesses
Country level	* Unstable macroeconomic environment.
* Stable political environment.	* Concerns about spillover from conflicts in African sub-continent.
* Significant growth potential.	
* Liberalized foreign exchange mechanism.	* Infrastructural weaknesses: transport, electricity (availability, reliability, cost).
* Unrestricted capital and dividend flows.	* Low productivity of labour.
* Proximity to European markets.	* Poorly organized employment market.
* Location as a "gateway" to West Africa.	* Difficult industrial relations.
* Preferential trade access via Cotonou and AGOA; member of ECOWAS.	* Deficient health services.
* Low-cost labour.	* Lack of "one-stop shop" for foreign investors.
* Perceived government commitment to business and foreign investment.	* Public conflicts between State shareholder and Ashanti Goldmines.
Sector and industry levels	
* Mining: exploration and extraction of gold, diamonds, bauxite and manganese.	* Mining: decline in world gold markets.
* Light manufacturing: trade preferences in garments sector; growth in handcrafts.	* Light manufacturing: poor design and quality; lack of clusters.
*Agriculture: abundant natural resources; growing markets in agro-processing; liberalization of cocoa industry.	*Agriculture: lack of a cold chain; poor transport within country; complex land ownership systems.
*Tourism: rapid growth, highly under-developed, and potential for variety of projects.	*Tourism: lack of infrastructure (hotel accommodation); unrest in region; lack of marketing.
* Utilities: privatization sales in all sectors of transport, telecoms, and energy.	* Utilities: lack of clear regulatory frameworks.
* Energy: boost to all sectors on the back of WAG pipeline; new oil exploration	* Energy: problems with tariff levels; concessions and anchor investors
Firm level	
	* Low standards of quality and control.
* Long-established TNCs.	* Relatively small formal sector.
*Wide-ranging concession and privatization programme.	* Lack of key skills and training, including management and marketing expertise.
* Low-cost labour.	* Low level of linkages between TNCs and domestic economy. Lack of networking.
* Specialized mine-engineering skills.	* Lack of entrepreneurship.

Source: UNCTAD Survey

Box III. 1. ACP-EU partnership agreement: Strengthening West Africa regional integration

The Cotonou Framework Agreement provides for the negotiation of new reciprocal trade agreements between the EU and the ACP countries. These agreements shall cover essentially all mutual trade, with few exceptions. ACP countries and the EU shall complete tariff removal within 10 years, unless specially justified. As the new trading arrangements are due to enter into force in December 2007, the European Commission aims at concluding negotiations of these arrangements by 2005.

The Cotonou Agreement provides instruments to promote investment in ACP countries, and to encourage joint ventures, co-financing and cooperation by European companies. To that effect, investment forums will be organized and an ACP- EU private sector business forum will be set up. The EU has pledged to provide long-term investment finance and risk capital, as well as technical support to mobilize domestic capital and encourage the flow of foreign capital; support specific investments; increase production and export competitiveness of ACP enterprises; and support the establishment of regional or national investment risk insurance schemes and guarantee programmes. The feasibility of setting up an ACP-EU Guarantee Agency will also be studied.

The regional dimension occupies a large place in the Cotonou Agreement, including structural adjustment programmes at the regional level, measures to promote regional integration, and compensation for costs of regional integration and budget revenue losses. On their part, ACP countries have agreed to introduce, within the economic partnership agreements, general principles on protection and promotion of investments.

The European Commission has proposed, as the main implementation form of the agreement, to conclude regional economic partnership agreements (REPAs) with the established regional integration groupings among the ACP countries, with the exception of new special LDC provisions (which extend, immediately, zero tariffs on all imports of all industrial and most agricultural products, except arms).

The Government of Ghana is pursuing the implementation of the REPA within ECOWAS, but progress has been slow in the start-up phase. Ghana should play a pivotal role in the negotiations, and take advantage of the new trade and investment potential offered by REPA..

Source: UNCTAD survey.

Table III. 4 Exports of agro-processed products, 1993-1999

(Millions of dollars)

Sector	1993	1994	1995	1996	1997	1998	1999	% change
Canned tuna	1.1	13.9	34.3	45.7	49.8	77.3	61.9	+ 5 527
Pineapples	5.2	5.3	5.6	10.9	9.6	8.8	13.0	+ 150
Cocoa products	35.4	25.2	28.2	60.4	91.6	79.0	55.1	+ 56

Source: World Bank (2001). *Ghana: International Competitiveness, Opportunities and Challenges Facing Non-Traditional Exports.* Report No. 22421-GH.

Ghana's comparative advantage for agro-processing investments include its supply of low-cost labour, its fertile soils and climate, and the particular trade privileges offered by the Cotonou Agreement. Exports of processed tuna, for example, increased from $1 million in 1993 to $77 million by 1998. They accounted for one fifth of total non-traditional exports, as FDI from firms such as Pioneer Food Cannery (affiliated to Heinz, United States) enabled entry into high-revenue markets in Europe. Untapped opportunities also exist to export fresh fish, which has much higher value than canned tuna.

In addition, Ghana has an impressive record in the export of fresh pineapples and canned pineapple juice. Ghana is the third largest exporter of fresh pineapples to the EU, and the largest to Switzerland, and has a positive track record in some of the world's most demanding markets (for example, Marks and Spencer and Sainsbury in the United Kingdom, which are known to have stringent health and environmental standards). Recent trade privileges have given Ghana an extra boost, and industry estimates indicate that production could increase at least fourfold.

The cocoa products market also appears to offer potential to investors, as Ghana's exports of cocoa products (cocoa paste, butter and liquor) have grown faster than traditional exports of cocoa beans. There is growing appreciation of the quality of Ghana's bitter-sweet chocolate in international gourmet markets. Ghana's presence in cocoa-product markets is still miniscule, especially considering that it produces top quality cocoa beans and is the world's second largest cocoa exporter. At present it serves only 1 per cent of the EU market for cocoa paste and 2 per cent for cocoa-powder, but the stronger examples set by neighbours such as Côte d'Ivoire and Cameroon should encourage Ghana.

FDI could help overcome some of the supply constraints in the agro-business sector. For example, enhanced development of the pineapple, horticultural, fresh fish and flower sectors will depend upon the construction of cold-storage facilities at Ghana's airports and ports and on improvement of the quality of feeder-roads between the agricultural and the agro-processing areas. The canning industry for both tuna and pineapples also requires further investment to improve technical standards, lower costs, and increase capacity. In the cocoa products sector, there is a need to reduce the dominant role of the State and to allow licensed private exporters equal access to warehousing and crop-financing. Finally, in all sectors, producers may benefit from encouraging the open-ended, negotiable contractual relationships that are being adopted between suppliers and high-quality global purchasers such as the Marks and Spencers supermarket chain. These help to provide more stability and guarantees to exporters, besides technical advice and capital.

(b) Light manufacturing

Light manufacturing has been a source of significant growth in employment and export revenues. Investors aiming at regional markets are attracted by Ghana's low operating costs compared to other ECOWAS competitors, its more reliable infrastructure and favourable fiscal incentives. Ghana has successfully exported aluminium and plastic products, foam mattresses, cotton fabrics, and hair products to the region – manufactured exports to the ECOWAS countries increased from $15 million in 1993 to over $87 million by 1999, and these industries will further benefit when low-cost power becomes available from the West Africa Gas Pipeline.

Investors aiming at global rather than regional markets have been attracted by Ghana's low-cost labour and its proximity and preferential entry to the United States and EU markets. Export success is notable in handicrafts, wood products and garments (table III.5). In 1990, Ghana earned three times more from the export of traditional logs and lumber than from wood products ($129 million compared to $36 million), but by 1999 earnings were roughly equal ($90 million compared to $85 million). Similarly, handicrafts have shown rapid growth, with exports almost tripling from $2.6 million in 1993 to $6.7 million by 1998.[36]

Table III. 5. Exports of light manufactured goods 1993-1999

(Millions of dollars)

Sector	1993	1994	1995	1996	1997	1998	1999	% change
Wood products	36.1	61.2	82.5	64.0	75.9	80.1	84.5	+ 134
Garments	0.8	1.8	1.7	0.3	0.6	5.2	2.7	+ 238

Source: World Bank (2001). *Ghana: International Competitiveness, Opportunities and Challenges Facing Non-Traditional Exports.* Report No. 22421-GH.

The rapid growth in exports of light manufactures hints at the potential that could be realized with further investment. The handicrafts sector, in particular, would benefit from investments that enhance the communication between producers and final users, to ensure that final products consistently meet consumer expectations. In addition, downstream forestry product processors need assurance of a timely and adequate supply of wood, a functioning auction system, and environmental certification of forest resources.

Ghana has established a modest presence in the garments sector over the last decade, but difficulties experienced by foreign investors (particularly in labour relations) resulted in pullouts. Further inflow of investment could come from the new advantages presented by the eight-year preferential access to the United States market recently accorded under AGOA (see box III.2). Its most significant aspects for Ghanaian textiles investors are:

♦ Lifting of all existing quotas on textiles products from sub-Saharan Africa;

♦ Extension of duty-free and quota-free market access for apparel manufactured from yarns and fabrics made in the United States, or not available in the United States; and

♦ Extension of duty-free and quote-free access for apparel made with African fabric and yarn, subject to a cap for eight years of 1.5-3.5 per cent of the total imports of apparel.

---

[36] World Bank (2001). Ibid

**Box III. 2. Attracting FDI under AGOA in Ghana
favours export development**

In October 2000, the United States African Growth and Opportunity Act (AGOA) designated 34 sub-Saharan African countries, including Ghana, as beneficiaries of special trade preferences. The purpose of AGOA is to strengthen United States relations with African countries, and to encourage African countries to pursue political and economic reforms and achieve higher economic growth. In sum, AGOA offers duty-free and quota-free United States market access for nearly all products through the existing Generalized System of Preferences (GSP) programme, ensured for at least eight years.

The potentially most significant aspects of AGOA to attract FDI in Ghana are those related to preferences for apparel and textile imports, including:

(a) the lifting of all existing quotas on textile products from sub-Saharan Africa;

(b) the extension of duty-free and quota-free United States market access for sub-Saharan African apparel made from yarns and fabrics either made in the United States or not available in the United States; and

(c) the extension of duty-free and quota-free United States market access for apparel made in Africa with African fabric and yarn, subject to a cap for eight years of 1.5-3.5 per cent of the total imports of apparel. (African countries with an annual GNP of less than $1,500, including Ghana, may use third-country fabric inputs for up to four years).

Also included in AGOA are cuts of fresh meat, prepared and preserved meats and fish, a variety of dairy products such as yoghurts, milk and cream products, butter and cheeses as well as fats and oils. Fruit and vegetables also get more complete duty-free access to the United States market, with many new fresh, frozen, dried, preserved or processed products being included as well as fruit juices and concentrates. In addition, wines and certain alcohols are covered, as are animal feed and tobacco products. Given the short implementation period of eight years, the Act will favour those countries that will take fast initiatives and those with existing business infrastructures. Export processing zones, for instance, that have attracted exporters in the past, now provide a haven for AGOA operators.

Source: : UNCTAD survey.

(c) Information technology and data processing

Ghana's endowments of skilled and low-cost labour would seem to offer potential in the information technology (IT) sector, the so-called "second generation starter industry" (as opposed to garments manufacture, which is a labour-intensive, "first generation" starter). Ghana does not yet have the communications and services clustering that characterizes the IT sector in the developed world. Nevertheless, investors may be encouraged by the positive experience of the first entrant in this sector (box III.3).

Box III. 3. Introducing high-technology computing and electronic processing

When ACS/BPS introduced its data-entry operations in Ghana in May 2000, it brought more computers into one site than had existed anywhere else in Ghana. It also introduced an entirely new kind of occupation, new methods of working, and a new system of piece-rate payment. In just a year of activity, the firm grew from 30 to 700 employees. The system works as follows: the headquarters of ACS/BPS, based in the United States, electronically sends scanned medical claim forms to Ghana, where over 700 clerks then input data by hand from the scanned images.

This has raised the salary and status of data entry clerks: they now typically earn between $100 and $200 per month, in a country where the local average income is closer to $32 per month. This is particularly noticeable given that 95 per cent of the staff is female. The system has also been claimed a success both for introducing new standards of expertise (since few typists could be found with the ability to type at 60 words per minute, free training was provided) and for its piece-work payment system, which had previously failed in other industries where it was introduced (particularly the garment industry). Other ripple effects include outsourcing of services, including transport, security, catering and training, as well as buying its computer hardware from local vendors. The firm plans to expand: to open another three sites and employ another 3,000 employees. One concern is its ability to find skilled labour, and to this end, it aims to tap into the student population of local universities and polytechnics. It has already developed an arrangement with Ghanaian secretarial colleges, teaching students to use its software.

Source: : UNCTAD survey.

(d) Tourism

Tourism is a young but expanding industry in Ghana. It currently contributes almost 4 per cent of GDP, and at the current annual growth rate of 12 per cent, tourism will soon be Ghana's main foreign exchange earner. Ghana's comparative advantage in this sector includes historical, cultural and archaeological sites that attract regional and international tourists (including Afro-Americans interested in Ghana's slavery history). Potential also exists for ecotourism. Recent signs that the new Ministry of Tourism will preserve important sites reinforce this sector's potential for investment. However, there are major constraints to be overcome, including Ghana's lack of infrastructure, marketing, and health and safety-related services and others that are important for tourists, such as tourist police and loss-recovery facilities. Tourism's infrastructure is weak, with few world-class hotels and almost no tourist-related services. Divestment of State-owned hotels could develop the potential of private sector investment and attract foreign investors with skills and expertise

(e) Mining and related services

There may be potential for further investment in the mining sector and, in particular, mining-related services, resource processing, resource extraction, and services in mining exploration. This could include, for example, investors with expertise in mine selection, mining sequencing and development planning. In addition, plans to upgrade the underground technology exploration programme in order to access new high-grade ore reserves at Obuasi may offer further opportunity, as may Ashanti Goldmine's outward investments in mining in Guinea, the United Republic of Tanzania and Zimbabwe. However, the sector is constrained by the fact that new investment has been declining due to Ghana's lagging competitiveness compared to other gold producers (for example, Australia, Canada and the United States, or the United Republic of Tanzania), and the decline in prices in global gold markets.

(f) Cocoa

Cocoa has long been a mainstay of the Ghanaian economy: it is a sector with a strong tradition of foreign investment. There is still some potential for foreign investors with a long-term horizon, but generally, the sector is constrained by falling world market prices, and the phasing out of the STABEX mechanism, following the introduction of the new Cotonou Agreement. One feature, which acts as both a constraint and an opportunity, is that only 15 per cent of Ghana's trees are currently in the peak output range, and there has been a long-term decline in new tree planting. Since there will be a significant fall in future cocoa production – barring dramatic increases in productivity, investors may be encouraged to plant new trees now, in order to exploit this future gap. The commitment of the COCOBOD State Marketing Board to license more exporting companies in the internal marketing system to ensure effective competition may also lead to increased FDI.

(g) Infrastructure

♦ Energy

There is potential for foreign investment to grow dramatically in Ghana's energy sector, given the Government's shift in policy stance towards more private sector involvement, capacity expansion and diversification from hydroelectric to other energy sources. If a number of critical obstacles are removed, new foreign investment could be on a very large scale. This could act as a catalyst for further investment throughout the entire economy - given the extent to which unreliable electricity supplies have slowed development. Shortages of electricity and water and uneconomic tariff levels, have proved to be a major constraint on investment in Ghana in all sectors (see box III.4).

The West African Gas (WAG) pipeline project for piping gas from Nigeria to Ghana, has the potential to become a critically important foreign investment. The $400 million project will involve a consortium led by Chevron, and including the Royal Dutch/Shell Group and national oil companies or other representative bodies from Nigeria, Togo, Benin and Ghana. However, to provide sufficient gas demand, some of the existing plants should convert to gas. The existing Takoradi plant, for example – designed to run on gas - currently runs on imported light crude oil.

There have also been a number of proposals for private, independent power-generating projects (IPPs). If the WAG project is successfully completed, it could also prompt a flurry of subsequent investments in IPPs. Investors that plan to use thermal fuel to run turbines will benefit from the construction of the WAG pipeline, which will reduce plant running and maintenance costs. Other potential investors await confirmation that they will be guaranteed access to the national grid. They also seek clarification on the future of the State-owned Electricity Corporation of Ghana, whose privatization has been delayed many times, and which would be a major customer for many of the private power plants. Potential investments in this category include, for example, a plant proposed in Tema.

New potential for foreign investors may lie in Ghana's offshore oil reserves. Dana Petroleum (United Kingdom) and Fusion Oil & Gas (Australia) have been conducting seismic studies offshore from Ghana; in March 2000, Dana struck a small oil find while drilling in shallow waters and is sinking a follow-up well in deeper waters. The discovery of commercial quantities of crude oil or gas would have a substantial effect on potential investment, which is likely to lead to increased FDI in oil exploration and extraction and also in the oil-services industries. The State-owned National Petroleum Corporation (GNPC) holds a minority stake in each exploration licence. Privatization of the national oil company would offer further potential for foreign investors.

Box III. 4. Volta Aluminium Company (Valco)

Valco is a critical firm for the Ghanaian economy. The firm exploits bauxite mining in Ghana and is vertically integrated into alumina production. Few countries in the world have bauxite, and production is highly concentrated because of the specific mining technology required. Bauxite mining in Ghana has a particular history. Valco was formed in the early 1960s as part of a larger financing deal for the construction of the Akosombo dam and its hydroelectric station. Negotiated by Presidents Kwame Nkrumah and John F. Kennedy in 1962, the United States, the United Kingdom, and the World Bank provided loans for the dam and the United States-based Kaiser Corporation (along with minority partner Reynolds) agreed to establish Valco. The company was to serve as the anchor energy customer for the project with a 50-year provision contract, thus both guaranteeing a steady income stream to help repay the loans and providing some investor confidence. Since it started production in 1967, Valco has continued to play an important role in the country's development.

With regard to employment, the company employs nearly 2,000 people when fully operational (recent power shortages have, however, led to reduced capacity and retrenchments). There is also an important indigenization component, and skills and linkages development. Over the years, the number of foreign workers has declined, from over 300 in the 1970s to about 10 today, with Ghanaians accounting now for about 99 per cent of total employees, including highly skilled engineers and technicians. As part of the agreement, a proportion of Valco's aluminium is retained inside the country for local processing. As a result, a handful of domestic aluminium firms have been established alongside Valco, including Aluworks (producing aluminium sheets and industrial /construction products) and Pioneer Aluminium (for consumer and household wares).

Valco's peculiar history is not without controversy; the following are important policy issues to be addressed. There are regular complaints about input content (i.e. that Kaiser uses alumina from its mines in Jamaica and elsewhere rather than using Ghanaian bauxite). Secondly, Valco retains only 10 per cent of its output for domestic industry, and there may be room to negotiate a higher level to encourage even greater expansion in domestic processing capacity. Energy provision is perhaps the most controversial aspect of the agreement. As part of the original contract, Valco was promised electricity at guaranteed rates.

This was seen as a necessary benefit to allow the project to move ahead; it is thus an indirect cost of financing electricity generation in Ghana for years to come. This provision for discounted energy rates has raised three issues in light of recent developments in the local energy sector. First, because energy costs are a substantial input cost for aluminium production, there are issues relating to the retention of relative competitiveness. Secondly, in light of recent power shortages, there are questions about the desirability of allowing one customer to take 30-45 per cent of Akosombo's power. Valco, which was legally entitled to full power allocation, did agree to some reductions and was forced to close some product lines. Finally, because Valco is one of the largest FDI undertakings in the country, it has a symbolic relevance with regard to investment guarantees provided to foreign investors in Ghana. Therefore, ongoing renegotiations for energy pricing between the Government and Valco need to strike a balance between meeting current developmental priorities and promoting the country as a competitive and safe destination for foreign-financed projects.

Source: : UNCTAD survey.

◆ Telecommunications

Ghana Telecom was partially privatized in 1996, with a 30 per cent stake sold to Telekom Malaysia. In February 2002, the Government abrogated its management contract with Telekom Malaysia and selected Telenor of Norway as management partner. The Government has signalled its intention to deregulate the sector, in the hope of attracting more operators. These are likely to be attracted to the landline network, rather than the over-subscribed, mobile telephone subsector (where five mobile licences were issued in a market of around 50,000 customers). Further potential for foreign investment may also reside in the Internet services market, where there are currently several private sector Internet Service providers (ISPs) (NCS being the market leader).

◆ Transport

Ghana's transport infrastructure currently poses a major constraint on investment and growth in all sectors; further FDI could be an effective way to resolve some of the problems associated with this, such as uncompetitive seaport charges and lengthy handling times, high airfreight cost and limited space, customs procedures and import/export clearing times. The Government plans to sell concessions to private investors in Ghana's main ports at Tema and Takoradi, as part of its Gateway strategy. This may attract foreign investors, especially those with specialized management and operations skills, who could raise profits by reducing Ghana's high port costs (table III.6). Ghana already has dockyard and ship repair facilities that could be developed into entrepôt hub activities for the region.

Table III. 6. West African comparative port charges for a 20,000 GT container vessel call*

(Thousands of dollars)

Tema	43 810
Lomé	39 785
Abidjan	18 322
Cotonou	8 773

* Average cost for full import/export of 200 20' and 100 40' containers, including all land and port charges.
Source: World Bank (2001). *Ghana: International Competitiveness, Opportunities and Challenges Facing Non-Traditional Exports.* Report No. 22421-GH.

Similarly, potential for foreign investment exists in the concessions to be offered in the railway system connecting Accra, Kumasi and Sekondi-Takoradi and in the future sale of Ghana Railways. In addition, the Government has committed itself to the eventual sale of the national carrier, Ghana Airways (although the schedule has been delayed several times and a new date has not been confirmed).

The potential of this sale to investors is enhanced by the fact that Kotoko International Airport in Accra is currently under major renovation; airport services have been leased to a private consortium led by a German company and these are expected to be well-equipped to cope with growing traffic volumes. Finally, foreign investors will have the opportunity to tender for government contracts to build and maintain Ghana's expanding national road network. Successful toll road projects, such as the highway linking Accra with Tema, suggest that there is potential for other similar "user-pays" schemes for private sector investors to build, own and/or operate.

B. Strategic Directions

Ghana's FDI potential extends beyond natural resources and includes a variety of industries, from agribusiness to information technology. Preferential trade agreements create market niches that may attract export-oriented FDI; in the longer term, local and regional markets could further catalyse FDI in manufacturing. Realizing this potential will require attention to key supply constraints.

1. Strengthen the Gateway strategy and link it to attracting FDI

Ghana has potential to attract export-oriented FDI in resource-based and labour-intensive industries for the global market. Manufactured exports aimed at market niches are favoured by AGOA. Negotiation for a regional partnership agreement with the EU within the new cooperation framework of ACP-EU could also provide Ghana with new trade and investment opportunities.

Ghana also has the potential to attract foreign investors seeking to establish manufacturing and service activities for the regional market. The market is weak and fragmented, and Ghana should firmly establish its position by further strengthening its regional trade arrangements. This includes renewing its commitment to enforce the ECOWAS trade liberalization scheme and moving forward on regional infrastructure projects. Ghana should also pursue agreements with its francophone neighbours (Togo, Burkina Faso and Côte d'Ivoire).

Ghana has engaged in a fast-track improvement of bilateral ties with Nigeria. Tariff harmonization between Ghana and Nigeria will soon come into effect, with monetary union formally planned for 2003. In addition to creating larger markets, which may serve as an inducement for foreign firms to locate manufacturing in Ghana, there is also the possibility of higher investment levels from larger Nigerian companies. Ghana is also committed to regional and multilateral integration, and such initiatives should support export diversification and attract FDI into new export-oriented investment.

To attract export-oriented FDI, Ghana needs to enhance its competitiveness and to position itself as a West African hub for import, export, storage, assembly, distribution, manufacturing, and trans-shipment of goods, services and passengers.

This is the aim of the Gateway project, which initiated regulatory reform and supported the development of FTZs (see box III.5). The project should be put on a fast track. As it enters its second phase of implementation, it should strengthen links between trade and investment promotion, particularly with respect to attracting FDI in infrastructure development.

Box III. 5. The Gateway Project

The Gateway Project aims to enhance Ghana's competitiveness and to position the country as a West African hub for import, export, storage, assembly, distribution, manufacturing, and trans-shipment of goods, services and passengers. The project has three main components:

- *Legislative, regulatory and incentives reform.* The project is an exercise to review customs practices and procedures and laws governing port services and aviation to ensure they are all up to international standards.

- *Capacity building.* Training of staff of the Customs, Excise and Preventive Services (CEPS), Ghana Immigration Service (GIS), Ghana Ports and Harbours Authority (GPHA), and the Ghana Investment Promotion Centre (GIPC).

- *Offsite infrastructure.* Financing for infrastructure development in the FTZs – especially water systems, electricity, telecommunications, sewage and waste treatment, roads construction, and rail links to Tema port.[37]

Source: Ministry of Trade.

Recommendations:

- **Establish bond-to-bond "hassle-free" land transport arrangements** with Governments of neighbouring countries, so that customs checks are done only at the bonded warehouse areas.

- **Initiate negotiations with neighbouring countries to set up "inland ports",** (government or private-sector-driven, or both) with joint ownership with the country involved. Accelerate the establishment of the proposed "shippers' council free inland port area" (under the Ghana Port and Harbour Authority) in Boankra.

- **Streamline import/export procedures in accordance with best practices of international standard**, and have each agency establish a "client charter" that is transparent and indicates time for every procedure.

(a) Free Trade Zones

The FTZ in Tema is threatening to become a white elephant; private developers/operators have difficulty attracting firms. One operator has 681 acres of developed land and several buildings, all unsold - another has approximately 210 acres (out of 250 acres) of unsold land. Yet there are plans to build another zone at Boankra. Despite the unutilized capacity, the Tema Development Corporation (TDC), which operates land outside the FTZ, and the Board have allowed "individual free zone enterprises" to set up just outside the fenced-off zone area. Moreover, the TDC sells land just outside the Tema Zone at $35,000 per acre, while the cost of land within the zone is higher. Ghana cannot afford to have developed land (either by the private sector or the Government) sitting idle. This is a drain on the economy and gives a bad impression to new investors coming to the country. Also there is a need for the Government to cater to industries that, over time, could develop into exporters and also to ancillary and supporting industries.

---

[37] Although the FTZs are privately financed, the Government is receiving technical assistance and other support from the World Bank for "trade facilitation services".

Recommendations:

◆ **Establish Multi-Facility Economic Zones (MFEZ).** The existing free zones and the non-zone areas in Tema should be transformed into industrial parks that provide options for modular design and standardized factory buildings, either for rent or sale; they should offer investors immediate project start-up and cluster firms inside the zones. The focus should be to attract labour-intensive projects into the zones. The transformed MFEZ could be jointly managed and promoted by the existing private sector establishments and relevant government agencies – an industrial park open both to domestic and foreign investors. If the experience was successful, the Boankra and Tokavadi/Sekordi areas could also be declared MFEZs or reserved for future declaration as MFEZs. A summary of the MFEZ concept is provided in box. III.6.

Box III. 6. The multi-facility economic zone concept

Multi-facility economic zones have proved successful in South-East Asia. Briefly, the concept is as follows: identify a substantial area (e.g. 1,000 hectares) and have an MFEZ Authority there working closely with private sector developers. Create best practice procedures for investors in this area at all levels – from project approval to production facilities. Establish world-class infrastructure (e.g. electricity, water and roads) in the zone. Provide housing for executives and workers, a hotel, a small township and recreation areas (if these not available nearby). Train local government officials on best practices from other existing specialized industrial zones. The MFEZ will cater for both export-oriented and domestic-oriented industries and thus save valuable land lying idle if the country is unable to attract 70 or 80 per cent of export-oriented industries. Introducing the MFEZ concept will require institutional adjustment. The present FTZ authority should be converted into the MFEZ authority, and be responsible, alone or in conjunction with the relevant local authorities, for development of the zone. The MFEZ authority becomes a one-stop centre for all "on the ground approvals", from land to building approvals, infrastructure and maintenance.

Source: UNCTAD

---

2. Reinforcing the SME sector

Ongoing initiatives to develop the entrepreneurial capacity in Ghana need to be continued and strengthened. Training and business support services, including access to information and finance, technology upgrading, and networking are necessary elements of such programmes. Initiatives by Empretec Ghana should also be strengthened.[38]

The export potential of SMEs would be greatly enhanced through the development of clusters that can build networks of production, distribution and/or technology and skills-sharing amongst firms. Certainly, the three sectors offering the most potential (agribusiness, tourism and information technology and data processing services) would benefit from a separate, more detailed, cluster-analysis study.

---

[38] Empretec began in Ghana in October 1990 as a project of the United Nations, Barclays Bank Ghana Limited and the Government of Ghana through the National Board for Small Scale Industries. In 1994, Empretec successfully transformed itself into a Foundation in order to enhance the sustainability of its programmes. Empretec Ghana currently has regional offices in Accra, Kumasi and Takoradi.

To tap FDI potential in Ghana, there is a need to develop a cluster approach to establish networks of production in key areas. Thus,

- Develop a broader agribusiness and food processing industry;
- Promote a tourism industry tapping Ghana's heritage, and develop ecotourism niches based on the changing trends in the world tourism market (see box III.7); and
- Attract FDI into information technology and build a network of suppliers and supporting institutions.

Box III. 7. Tourism policies

The formulation of policies for attracting the private sector in general, and FDI in particular, to harness the country's tourism potential has become a priority for the Government. The development of two key resort areas, which could become models of best practices, might attract FDI. The following measures could be introduced:

- A strong private-public sector partnership for tourism infrastructure development;
- Private management of hotels;
- Establishment of a well-built regulatory agency to introduce standards and quality control, and preservation of national and world heritage sites;
- Issuance of certification, control and monitoring by a joint public-private agency;
- Establishment of a tourist police and health emergency services for tourists;
- Establishment of specialized schools in cooperation with the private sector; and
- Targeted promotion with a clear market focus.

The Ministry of Tourism is encouraging all stakeholders in the tourism industry to increase efforts to market tourism in order to generate more employment revenue. A new proposal has been submitted by the Minister of Tourism to generate revenue from visitors as a tourism development and promotion levy, with 80 per cent of all attraction fees at national museums and heritage sites to be kept for use at the site where they are generated. However, there are other financial tools that could be explored to raise money for conservation while at the same time developing the tourism industry. Innovative contracts for private sector service provisions in protected areas should be explored as an alternative to levies.

Source: UNCTAD survey.

Ghana does not possess a strong array of businesses to build successful clusters. Without a strong domestic business sector to act as partner, supplier and/or customer, FDI potential cannot be realized. To develop a cluster approach, Ghana needs to create a hospitable environment for start-ups and SMEs, which could become partners with foreign investors as suppliers of goods and services. Outsourcing could translate into stable, long-term, multi-year contracts with TNCs, thereby building linkages and catalysing domestic entrepreneurship. Foreign investors could also take a proactive role in promoting linkages with domestic enterprises, and thus nurture SME development. Existing SME development programmes, including Empretec Ghana, should participate in this endeavour to promote linkages.

Three schemes are proposed:

- Small aggregation initiative for SME development.
- Incubators for SME development.
- Microenterprises programmes.

The proposed schemes are as follows:

(a) Small Aggregation Initiative (SAI) for SME Development

Small aggregation enables SMEs to expand and address their financing needs, to upgrade managerial skills, and to cope with the limited production capacity and other constraints. This concept is not new to Ghana; for example, the Kumasi Magasin – an agglomeration of informal panel-beating and car repair shops – has existed for over 20 years, driven by the need to take advantage of pooled resources to access land, and for group purchasing, pooling of tools, information-sharing and cooperating to meet customers' demands in terms of quantity, price or delivery time.

The Small Aggregation Initiative (SAI) for SME Development should focus on developing complementary production schemes and forming joint ventures geared to expansion and modernization. If three companies are brought together – each can take 30 per cent equity, and the remaining 10 per cent share can be held by a coordinator. The role of coordinator could be played by a TNC or by a small board of stakeholders and support institutions, including the private sector, TNCs, donors, Empretec Ghana and GIPC. The scheme should cater to activities that have similar needs for machinery, but where the end products are different and non-competing, such as manufacturing of aluminium or stainless steel products (e.g. ranging from cups, saucers and plates to items for office and industrial use). Equipment for the initial production process would be similar (e.g. presses, cutting and bending machines) but the end product would be different. The same scheme could apply to the manufacturing of wooden furniture, including home and office supplies. Initial machinery would be similar – for sawing, planing and shaping – but the production process for the end product would be different.

Such joint-venture schemes can allow:
♦ Purchase or rental of a bigger building;
♦ Bulk purchase of modern machinery, equipment and raw materials;
♦ Hiring of a skilled manager and other staff;
♦ Access to loans from banks; and
♦ Developing outsourcing in production of components and services for TNCs operating in Ghana or in West Africa.

The Small Aggregation Initiative (SAI) for SME Development should start as a pilot programme in selected sectors. TNCs should be encouraged to play the role of coordinator, particularly when outsourcing can be developed. TNCs can provide concrete information on subcontracting requirements (i.e. on quantities, time delivery and quality).

(b) Incubators for SME development

Start-up SMEs require ongoing, tailor-made assistance for every aspect of business development and management. Some existing programmes, such as Empretec Ghana, assist SMEs during the start-up and expansion phases of the business but are not located in one premise and do not focus on specific sectors (incubators without walls). Another concept for providing technical and managerial support for a defined time period, is the smart building concept. It houses SMEs in specialized centres, incubating the business while providing production and retail facilities.

There are good examples of incubators that focus on similar types of products or technology, which benefit from their proximity to and input from TNCs in the target sector:

◆ Incubator facilities can be established in target areas. They can be multi-storey buildings of average-sized units adequate for SME operations, including trading, workshops, assembly and printing facilities.

◆ A Central Service Facility (CSF) can offer a quick start-up service. The CSF should provide a telephone, fax, computer facilities and secretarial assistance. These services should be provided on a fee basis, according to their use.

◆ A facilitator, or well-trained, dynamic manager, should manage the centre and assist all SMEs in the start-up phase, in matters such as introduction to banks and credit facilities, assisting with marketing and accounting.

◆ The incubator should provide case-by-case technology advice and information on standards and quality requirements, in cooperation with technology institutions, practitioners and TNCs.

◆ GIPC could provide the incubators with institutional support including education, training and technical advice to manufacturers, modelled, for example, on the network support system established by the Jamaica Investment Promotion Agency in Jamaica.[39]

(c) Micro-enterprises Programme

In order to mobilize Ghana's entrepreneurial potential, the country needs to develop a strong base of micro-enterprises. Aid-sponsored programmes in Ghana already promote the growth of private-sector-led non-traditional exports through the micro-enterprise sector. Such programmes could also encourage the formation of micro-enterprise associations - which could then benefit from legal support in securing business licences, credit facilitation, and specific training programmes to develop supply capabilities and improve quality standards. New programmes could include:

◆ Introducing contract farming to intensify small-scale agriculture, and encouraging linkages between producers and buyers.

◆ Strengthening the linkages between GIPC and organizations that provide services to the microenterprises sector to increase their capacity, outreach, scale, sustainability, and service quality.

◆ Establishment of an "investment production village programme", based on the existing and successful experience in the trade area, which would develop subcontracting or outsourcing networks in the villages.

3. Technology and education policies

Ghana has the potential to produce world-class products in resource-based and labour-intensive industries for the global market. However, existing industrial capabilities are adequate mainly for primary production and simple processing. Upgrading of the manufacturing base to support world-class products will require a comprehensive strategy centred on improvement of local skills, assimilation of new technology and skills, and the strengthening of institutional support for the transfer and adaptation of new technologies. Also needed is a strategy to stimulate technology demand within the industrial sector, to monitor industrial needs and to link research and development (R&D) to industry and manufacturing requirements.

---

[39] The Jamaica Investment Promotion Agency (JAMPRO) hosts a productivity centre for SMEs and has also established an institutional support network for SMEs in garments and information technology. For example, in garments, JAMPRO sponsors a design centre and apparel technical centres for SMEs.

In the 1990s, there has been little investment in capital goods. Capacity utilization has risen marginally and technical efficiency has remained low. A firm-level comparison indicates that labour productivity (value added per employee) in Ghana's manufacturing sector is three times lower than in Cameroon, Kenya and Zimbabwe (Bigsten, 2000).[40] Although the wage level in Ghana is much lower than in Mauritius, the unit cost of production, or productivity-weighted wages, is higher. Thus the wage level in Ghanaian firms is uncompetitive. The root cause of this problem can be traced to the science and technology (S&T) system, and its limited capacity to transfer, use and adapt imported technology effectively.

There is a long-standing national recognition of the importance of science and technology in national development, dating back to research institutions set up by the colonial administrators. The Ministry of Environment, Science and Technology (MEST) heads the current policy-making structure - which is fragmented and comprises mainly public institutions that have few links with the productive sectors (see figure III.1).

Within the Ministry, the Council for Scientific and Industrial Research is responsible for S&T policy. Policy proposals by the Council include financing of R&D at the enterprise level and other support for the acquisition, assessment, adaptation, adoption and application of essential technology for industrial development. To date, however, these objectives remain unfulfilled. The S&T institutional infrastructure needs to be transformed into a national innovation system.

Recommendations:

◆ **Undertake a "technology foresight" exercise** with a view to assessing local technological competence by global standards. Many industrialized and newly industrialized countries have set up "technology foresight" programmes - developed with all parties concerned with science and technology: industrial leaders and researchers, academia, services, financial institutions and the government. The strength of such programmes lies in the consultation process, which creates awareness of the importance of technological competitiveness.

It also allows for an overall evaluation of the strengths and weaknesses of national innovation systems, builds consensus for carrying out a common plan of action, and facilitates the mobilization of resources and commitment. An exercise for Ghana can be modelled on the experience of other developing countries and adapted to Ghana's needs and technological conditions.

It should lead to more effective S&T policies and actions, including upgrading of technical skills and capabilities, strengthening S&T-related institutions and promoting entrepreneurial skills.

---

[40] Bigsten et al (2000). *Rates of return on physical and human capital in Africa's manufacturing sector.* Economic Development and Cultural Change, vol. 48 (4): 801-827.

Figure III.1. The Science and Technology System in Ghana

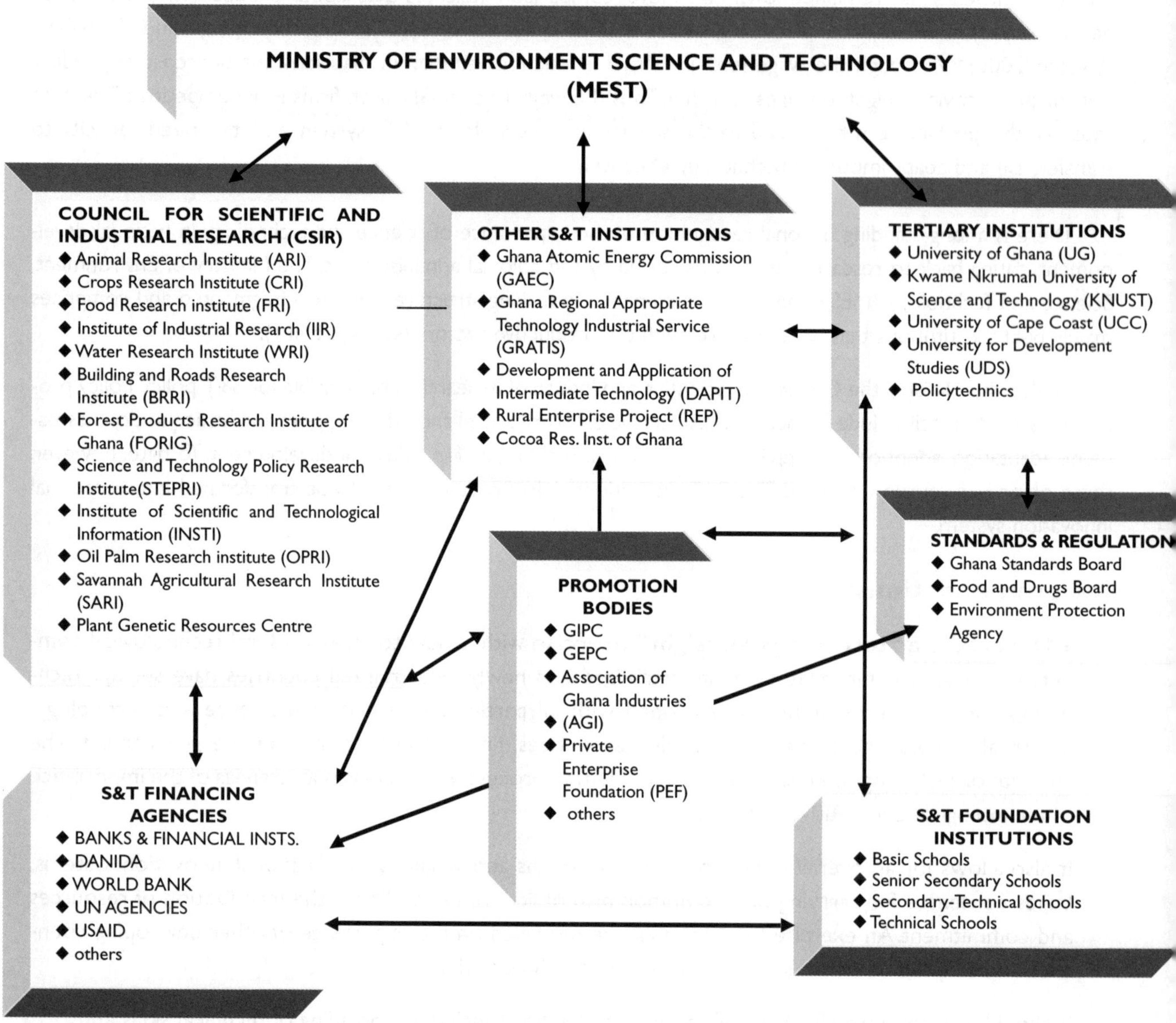

MINISTRY OF ENVIRONMENT SCIENCE AND TECHNOLOGY (MEST)

COUNCIL FOR SCIENTIFIC AND INDUSTRIAL RESEARCH (CSIR)
- Animal Research Institute (ARI)
- Crops Research Institute (CRI)
- Food Research institute (FRI)
- Institute of Industrial Research (IIR)
- Water Research Institute (WRI)
- Building and Roads Research Institute (BRRI)
- Forest Products Research Institute of Ghana (FORIG)
- Science and Technology Policy Research Institute(STEPRI)
- Institute of Scientific and Technological Information (INSTI)
- Oil Palm Research institute (OPRI)
- Savannah Agricultural Research Institute (SARI)
- Plant Genetic Resources Centre

OTHER S&T INSTITUTIONS
- Ghana Atomic Energy Commission (GAEC)
- Ghana Regional Appropriate Technology Industrial Service (GRATIS)
- Development and Application of Intermediate Technology (DAPIT)
- Rural Enterprise Project (REP)
- Cocoa Res. Inst. of Ghana

TERTIARY INSTITUTIONS
- University of Ghana (UG)
- Kwame Nkrumah University of Science and Technology (KNUST)
- University of Cape Coast (UCC)
- University for Development Studies (UDS)
- Policytechnics

PROMOTION BODIES
- GIPC
- GEPC
- Association of Ghana Industries
- (AGI)
- Private Enterprise Foundation (PEF)
- others

STANDARDS & REGULATION
- Ghana Standards Board
- Food and Drugs Board
- Environment Protection Agency

S&T FINANCING AGENCIES
- BANKS & FINANCIAL INSTS.
- DANIDA
- WORLD BANK
- UN AGENCIES
- USAID
- others

S&T FOUNDATION INSTITUTIONS
- Basic Schools
- Senior Secondary Schools
- Secondary-Technical Schools
- Technical Schools

Source: : UNCTAD (forthcoming). Transfer of Technology Policies – Case Studies of Ghana, Kenya, Tanzania and Uganda.

- **Strengthen the institutions dealing with quality control and standards,** and envisage collaboration with industry in the monitoring of such standards. Ensure the training of local staff in ISO certification of the International Organization for Standardization. Emphasize the importance of quality standards and control, particularly in SMEs. The Ghana Standards Board should play a central role in such efforts. In spite of budgetary and technical constraints, the Board has made some achievements, such as appointment by the EU to inspect facilities, test products and issue health certificates for the export of fish and fishery products to the EU market.

(a) Technical skills

There is a shortage of appropriate skills in the Ghanaian labour market, despite high unemployment (19 per cent in 2000) and the fact that the population is reasonably well educated by African standards. Ghana has a low illiteracy rate (32.2 per cent) compared to Senegal (65.5) and Nigeria (40.4), and the duration of compulsory primary education is greater than the African average. Ghana also has a higher rate of secondary level enrolment than Kenya, the United Republic of Tanzania and Uganda; however, in terms of technical education, as measured by the engineering enrolment index, Ghana performs worse. TNCs often find that the average Ghanaian university graduate lacks the kind of exposure to international standards they require.[41] Other areas of concern are lack of labour market information and lack of institutional and private sector mechanisms for placement of trained personnel.[42] For example, there are no employment agencies in the country.

Technical and vocational education is lacking in key areas, such as accounting, information technology and management. Specialized institutions have been established, including the Tarkwa School of Mining, Kwadaso Agricultural College, and Bunso Cocoa College. However, these institutions lack funds and assistance could possibly be sought, from mining companies for the Tarkwa School of Mining. A regional effort through the Association of African Universities (AAU), established in Accra 1967, envisages cooperation among African universities for the improvement of curricula, and the enhancement of training and management of institutions, improving R&D and improving the position of women in tertiary education, with an emphasis on information and communications technologies within institutions.

Recommendations:

- ◆ **Provide incentives for firms** to undertake quality training programmes that go beyond their immediate job needs. About two thirds of Ghana's industrial workers receive formal structured training, either in-house or outside. In-house training, however, does not seem to have had an immediate impact on productivity and wages. Incentives (cost deduction from taxable income) should be based on both demand and supply. There is a need to strengthen the fiscal incentives for training expenditures and to advocate the use of quality or specialized training institutes or private training consultants and to strengthen training institutions, particularly with a view to adapting focus and programmes to the needs of the industrial sector.

- ◆ Joint private-public financing schemes should be introduced to upgrade training in secondary and tertiary education as well as in technical schools.

- ◆ Establish an employment agency. This could be a joint public/private sector effort. Such an agency could operate both at national and regional levels, offering services such as registration of the unemployed, training and recruitment services to ECOWAS member countries. The agency should regularly hold regional job fairs – which could facilitate entry level recruiting for corporations – and promote regional training programmes.

---

[41] In the private sector, the following skills have been found to be in short supply: production and materials management, accounting and financial management, marketing, statistics, auditing, civil, electrical and mechanical engineering, personnel management and information management (ILO survey conducted in 2001, forthcoming).

[42] Kwabia Boateng (1996). *Employment, Unemployment and Underemployment in Ghana*. Institute of Economic Affairs, Occasional Paper, No.3, Accra: IEA.

4. Privatization and infrastructure development

The privatization programme in Ghana has attracted FDI and contributed to modernizing SOEs. Up to 2001, the divestiture of 233 SOEs (or parts of them) had been authorized by the President's Office. In some areas, however, privatization has been slow to achieve the expected benefits because of weaknesses in the regulatory regime, as outlined in chapter II. The new Government is committed to putting the privatization programme on a fast track and to improving its results. In order to enhance the privatization programme and bring about the benefits of improved quality, range and coverage of services, the following should be considered:

- In public utilities, management could be privatized without privatizing ownership of the assets. Management contracts, leases and concessions have been used successfully the world over, particularly in sectors where it is difficult to attract private investors.

- Some SOEs require pre-sale restructuring and plans to tender services as an interim step before privatization;

- Introduce competition by enacting a competition law and strengthen independent regulatory authorities – or establish them if they do not already exist – to monitor prices, investment commitments and incentives.

- Address social and distributive issues (for example, ensure coverage and introduce a special tariff for low-income users) as part of the contract negotiations.[43]

There are a number of reports that have assessed the resources gap and possible modalities to involve private sector financing for infrastructure development. The Government is currently focusing on expanding infrastructure to rural areas in the context of its poverty reduction programme. This does not contradict the aim of increasing private sector participation in project financing, as improvements in rural areas are also critical in order to upgrade supply capacity. Besides specific improvements in the regulatory framework already reviewed in chapter II, the following, relevant in the context of attracting FDI, may be considered.

Tema and Takoradi ports. To promote private participation in ports, there is a need to develop a specific implementation plan to assess the necessary corporate structure to manage the ports and determine the nature of services and facilities they should provide.

Railways and roads. The use of concessions has been successfully employed in only a few cases. The preparation of guidelines on concession and the establishment of procedures could encourage their use.

Water. The Government plans to lease the operation, maintenance and management of the water supply system. Issues related to a possible negative impact on cost and access for poor households and rural communities have been raised. A public-private sector partnership in management should also involve the commitment to renewal and expansion investment to ensure access to safe and affordable water. Privatising water should not be based on short-term financial considerations.

Air transport. There is a need to develop regulations for implementation of a liberal skies policy, and divestiture of the national carrier is under consideration.

---

[43] In Peru, for example, telecom companies offer "popular lines" which have no connection fee and a flat monthly rate for limited traffic; this is attractive for poor households with limited telephone usage.

Telecommunications. Service and infrastructure providers should preferably be separated, and they should concentrate on their respective competencies while maintaining commercial relations with each other. As already suggested, the regulatory capacity of the National Communications Authority should be strengthened (see chapter II) to enable it to respond adequately to the needs of the private telecom operators.

Energy. In electricity, the success of most independent power projects (IPPs) will depend on the ability of the producers to secure access to the grid for transmission. The reform action plan issued by the Government already envisages "open access" and the establishment of transparent guidelines for tariff setting. The planned regional integration scheme for energy also counts on efficiency improvements and cooperation with participating agencies. Other priorities include training regional power officials and establishing a comprehensive regional data bank on demand and capacity trends. The Government also wishes to facilitate further divestiture in energy services. In oil, the Government is establishing improved terms for oil exploration as part of a wide-ranging reform of the petroleum sector that includes restructuring Ghana National Petroleum Corporation to concentrate on exploration and production.

5. Investment promotion

The privatization programme in Ghana has attracted FDI and contributed to modernizing SOEs. Up to 2001, the divestiture of 233 SOEs (or parts of them) had been authorized by the President's Office. In some areas, however, privatization has been slow to achieve the expected benefits because of weaknesses in the regulatory regime, as outlined in chapter II. The new Government is committed to putting the privatization programme on a fast track and to improving its results. In order to enhance the privatization programme and bring about the benefits of improved quality, range and coverage of services, the following should be considered:

- GIPC is a well-established institution in Ghana and it has a good track record in many areas. It has been proactive in investor targeting, and devised successful campaigns to attract Asian investors as well as the Home-Coming Summit for non-resident Ghanaians. To put a future investment promotion strategy within the overall context of private sector development, the following priorities for the short and medium terms are suggested:

- Investment promotion in the next three years should focus on existing investors. GIPC should spell out an action programme to revive domestic and established foreign investor activity. This requires a coordinated contribution from a number of different public and private sector institutions to develop integrated policies. The strategy should focus on investment generation and servicing activities.

- GIPC should function as a one-stop service that provides assistance to foreign investors for obtaining the requisite authorizations, licences and permits (including land acquisition) from the authorities concerned. It should establish investment servicing at the national and regional levels.

- "Package" a number of privatization opportunities, providing details such as opportunities, potential and incentives/facilities offered. It is proposed that after several privatization projects have been duly "packaged" to offer good commercial propositions to investors, Ghana should launch a major promotional initiative, by holding Privatization Potential Seminars in key economies in East Asia and other regions. The existing Asia Africa Investment Technology Promotion Centre (AAITPC) located in Kuala Lumpur (Malaysia), which is a UNIDO initiative funded by the Japanese Government, is one such vehicle that could help with this kind of proactive promotion in Asia.

- Promote linkages between foreign investors and domestic suppliers. To this end, GIPC should work closely with existing institutions in support of SME development. It should help build market knowledge on cluster opportunities for local enterprises in Ghana, but also in West Africa, and promote the establishment of an "outward investment" service to encourage local entrepreneurs to think regionally and enter into joint ventures with ECOWAS partners.

- Establish institutional links between the Ghana Export Promotion Council, Ghana Free Zone Board and GIPC. Strengthen GIPC's role in export-oriented investment promotion, bringing under a single umbrella programme the Ghana Export Promotion Council and Ghana Free Zone Board to target investments in new export- oriented areas such as information technology. The reconfiguration of these institutions and their consolidation into one single agency should be considered.

C. Conclusion

Ghana is well endowed with many valuable natural resources, and is strategically well placed for access to markets in Europe and the rest of Africa. Investors can benefit from increased regional integration - which opens new potential linkages throughout West Africa - beyond the traditional boundaries that previously separated the region. They can also benefit from recent measures for improved access to markets in Europe and the United States.

The proposed reduction of tariffs between countries in the region and the new multilateral and bilateral agreements are expected to boost trade. The streamlining of import/export procedures and the implementation of other reforms by the Gateway Project are underway, which will strengthen existing linkages between FDI and trade.

In attracting FDI, however, Ghana needs to encourage domestic growth and foster linkages, particularly between TNCs and SMEs. To develop clusters in the main sectors with FDI potential, effective linkages and synergies need to be created. Policy measures to facilitate cluster establishment may include specific programmes to set up partnership schemes between SMEs and TNCs, develop incubators, and initiate microenterprise development programmes. The upgrading of free zones into industrial parks would also induce the geographic concentration of exporters, thereby enhancing horizontal linkages. A change in policy tack is also needed in the area of education and S&T for the development of skilled, adaptive and innovative human resources. Education and S&T should be more focused so as to respond to the needs of the private sector.

Joint private-public sector schemes should be encouraged to support entrepreneurship (see table III.7).

A well-maintained physical infrastructure is crucial to FDI development. The capital investment required for infrastructure upgrading needs the increased participation of private investors in project financing. In regard to privatization of public utilities (to ensure a sound sequencing of liberalization) a corollary regulatory framework needs to be devised and implemented - especially in the areas where only privatization of management can be sought. Telecommunications and power are two sectors are frequent targets of complaint by foreign and domestic investors; both are undergoing difficult transitions and a stronger regulatory framework is needed. These sectors, along with oil exploration, appear to hold great potential for attracting FDI if the policy and regulatory environment can be improved.

Regarding the investment promotion strategy, the Government should reinforce private-public sector dialogue and strengthen the institutional links for GIPC to act as a "one-stop centre". GIPC's core activities should be investment generation and servicing; it should encourage clustering in key sectors and provide institutional support involving education, training and technical advice to both local and foreign investors.

Table III. 7. Policy measures to attract FDI to Ghana

	OBJECTIVES		
	Cluster development	**Regional exports**	**Global exports**
Key sectors	• Agribusiness • Information technology • Tourism	• Agribusiness • Services • Electrical appliances • Metal/plastic products • Cosmetics	• Agribusiness • Garments • Tourism • Mining • Information technology
Type of investment	• Joint ventures • Outsourcing • Strategic alliances with TNCs	• Sequential investments by established TNCs • Joint ventures • Franchising/licensing • Greenfield	• Greenfield • Joint ventures • Subcontracting
Market potential	• Geographical mandates • Niche markets (e.g. ecotourism and organic food)	• Preferential access to: • ECOWAS • Nigeria • Communauté francaise africaine (CFA) Zone	• Preferential access to: • United States under AGOA • EU
Policy measures	• SAI/incubation centres for SMEs • Education/Technology • Infrastructure development • Strengthening the Gateway Project • Upgrading FTZs into MFEZs • Target promotion	• Infrastructure upgrading • Technology development • Outward investment • Education & Training • Strengthening the Gateway Project • Upgrading FTZs into MFEZs • Target promotion	• Infrastructure upgrading • Technology development • Education & Training • Strengthening the Gateway Project • Upgrading FTZs into MFEZs • Target promotion

Source: UNCTAD

IV. Main Conclusions and Recommendations

Ghana clearly has the potential to regain its position as a front runner in Africa for FDI. However, it needs to recover lost ground: improvements in economic performance needs to be sustained and remnants of the prolonged economic crisis removed. Macroeconomic instability, weak infrastructure, low productivity and lack of local business partners, all deter FDI. Several wide-ranging actions are needed to restore investor confidence

Objective 1. Improve the investment framework

The investment framework is generally sound and provides for non-discriminatory treatment and guarantees to investors. However, some of the provisions crafted 10 years ago no longer respond to new concerns. Areas for suggested reforms are:

- ◆ Review provisions of the 1994 Investment Code with a view to easing company establishment and ownership restrictions by sectors (chapter II, A.1.);

- ◆ Initiate new BITs and DTTs and ratify existing ones with all target countries (chapter II, A.2);

- ◆ Place the tax system on an equal footing with international standards, particularly withholding tax, tax auditing and tax administration (chapter II, B.1.);

- ◆ Strengthen consultation with the private sector (including labour unions) to improve labour dispute settlement mechanisms and facilitate flexible working hours, in line with best practices in other successful developing countries (chapter II, B.3.);

- ◆ Establish a task force to reform land laws, and facilitate foreign/domestic, freehold or leasehold ownership by the establishment of land banks coordinated by GIPC (chapter II, B.6.); and

- ◆ Reinforce the regulatory framework and institutions dealing with infrastructure development and privatization (chapter II, D.4).

Objective 2. Launch a "booster programme"

Ghana needs a booster programme to revive investment by domestic and established foreign investors. The booster programme should include supply-side actions to encourage expansion of existing businesses and reinvestment by existing investors in new projects; the latter, in turn, will attract new FDI.

The booster programme should address issues that can be reviewed and implemented within six months to one year, with concrete results envisaged over a three-year time frame.

- The recently established Investors' Advisory Council identified areas for action.[44] In finance, a task force will examine how venture capital and a development bank can improve financing for exporters and SMEs. A proposal that deserves quick follow-up is expansion of the private Enterprise Export Development Fund and the Trade and Investment Promotion Fund.

- Review tariff structure and remove inconsistencies. A special task force, headed by the Ministry of Finance and composed of representatives of the Ministry of Trade, GIPC and the private sector, should be set up to remove anomalies in the structure of import duty that discriminates against local assemblers and manufacturers.

- Encourage existing manufacturers to expand and diversify. All new investments in production capacity could get accelerated depreciation allowance that allows write-off within three years.

- Remove infrastructure bottlenecks faced by the private sector, and, where the Government is unable to provide support, offer a 100 per cent investment allowance, to be offset against profits for "approved infrastructure development" undertaken by the private sector.

- Introduce off-peak electricity tariff rates to encourage manufacturers to move production processes away from peak periods in order to overcome shortages and breakdowns due to strains on existing electricity grids.

- On-the-job training should be encouraged and companies providing it could be offered fiscal incentives (cost deduction from taxable income).

- "Package" slated privatization offerings that include providing details of opportunities, potential and incentives/facilities offered. After several privatization projects have been duly "packaged" offering investors good commercial propositions, GIPC could launch a major promotional initiative, by holding Privatization Potential Seminars in key economies in East Asia and other regions.

Objective 3.   Strengthen the Gateway strategy, and link it to attracting FDI

The Gateway Project should establish clear links with investment promotion, including the involvement of GIPC in design and reform implementation. A government-private sector task force should examine the following recommendations (chapter III, B.1):

(a) Establish Ghana as the major West African hub for trading and entrepôt activities

- Establish bond-to-bond "hassle-free" land transport links with neighbouring countries, so that customs checks are only at the bonded warehouse areas;

- Since establishing an efficient land transport system could be a longer-term objective, encouraging the set-up of cargo ferries to increase sea transport to neighbouring countries would reduce dependence on emerging land transport systems;

- Initiate negotiations with neighbouring countries to set up inland ports (administered by the Government or the private sector), with joint ownership by the countries involved;

---

[44] These areas are: land reforms, mining laws, labour laws, safety and security, infrastructure development in energy, telecommunications, information technology, financial service infrastructure, public sector sensitivity to the private sector, restoring the mining sector to competitiveness, re-orienting the economy from commodity and aid-dependency to a more diversified one and promoting partnerships between the Government, the private sector and industries' labour. See: www.gipc.org.gh/IPA.

◆ Accelerate the establishment of the proposed Shippers' Council Free Inland Port Area (under the Ghana Port and Harbour Authority) in Boankra.

(b) Establish Ghana as a centre for regional maritime engineering, technology and services

◆ Attract FDI to maximize Ghana's existing position/strengths in shipbuilding and repair by creating a cluster of maritime-based economic activities to serve domestic and regional needs.

(c) Set up Multi-Facility Economic Zones

◆ To forestall the possibilities of the existing FTZs in Ghana not contributing effectively to Ghana's economic recovery programme, consider the establishment of the multi-facility economic zones, as recommended (chapter III. B.1.).

Objective 4. Support SMEs

Ongoing initiatives to develop entrepreneurial capacity in Ghana need to be strengthened. The export potential of SMEs would be enhanced by the development of clusters. Cluster potential should be reviewed by sector, in collaboration with the private sector and research institutions. The development of domestic initiatives, especially the development of SMEs, should be given priority. Large foreign and domestic firms could promote linkages with domestic enterprises. Three schemes are proposed:

◆ **Small Aggregation Initiative for SME Development:** SMEs should develop complementary production schemes and form joint ventures geared to expansion and modernization. If three companies are brought together, each could take 30 per cent equity, and the remaining 10 per cent share could be held by a coordinator. The role of coordinator could be played by the private sector or by a small board of stakeholders and support institutions, including the private sector, TNCs, donors, Empretec Ghana and GIPC.

◆ **Incubators for SME Development:** Incubator facilities can be multi-storey buildings of average-sized units adequate for SME operations. The smart building concept can be useful to provide SMEs with specialized centres that act as incubators for them, providing production as well as retail spaces. A central service facility (CSF) could offer a quick start-up service.

◆ **Microenterprises programmes:** Aid-sponsored programmes in Ghana have promoted the growth of private-sector-led non-traditional exports through the micro-enterprise sector. Such programmes encourage the creation of micro-enterprises' associations that benefit from legal support in securing business licences, credit facilitation, and specific training programmes to develop supply capabilities and improve quality standards. GIPC should strengthen its links with organizations that provide services to the micro-enterprises sector.

Objective 5.   Develop human resources and technology policies

◆ A public-private sector partnership should be developed with the aim of enhancing labour skills, and incentives provided for firms to undertake quality training programmes (chapter III, B.3.).

◆ Encourage the establishment in Ghana of private-sector educational institutions that offer "twinning programmes" (e.g. with foreign university/college degrees awarded within Ghana) to make the country a regional centre of educational excellence. Appropriate support facilities/incentives should be considered in order to attract FDI into the sector (chapter III, B.3.).

◆ Joint private-public financing schemes could be set up to upgrade training in secondary and tertiary education as well as in technical schools (chapter III, B.3.).

◆ Establish an employment agency (possibly as a joint public/private sector effort), which could operate at both the national and regional level and offer services to ECOWAS member countries. Its functions would be to register the unemployed, gather information on skills and education and provide recruitment services and training. The agency could hold regular regional job fairs to facilitate entry level recruitment for corporations, and it could promote regional training programmes (chapter III, B.3.).

◆ Undertake a "technology-foresight" exercise with a view to assessing Ghana's local technological competence by global standards (chapter III, B.3.).

◆ Provide support and appropriate incentive schemes for collaboration and initiate a network that brings together private sector and government R&D institutions (chapter III, B.3.).

◆ The Ministry of Environment, Science and Technology could play a key role in implementing the national R&D policy by coordinating between the different public institutions involved and the private sector. It could also raise financing by commercializing new R&D. R&D institutions need to attract well-qualified personnel by offering salary schemes comparable to those of the private sector (chapter III, B.3.).

◆ Selection of priority technology areas for R&D must be based on enterprises' needs, linking S&T to other policy domains (trade, investment, education, environment and health). Direct incentives could be offered to enterprises for the use of advanced technology (chapter III, B.3.).

◆ Strengthen the institutions dealing with quality control and standards, and involve industry in the monitoring of such standards. Ensure the training of local staff in ISO certification.

Objective 6. Strengthen investment promotion

Based on Ghana's recent experience with investment promotion, the following institutional aspects should be considered (chapter III.B.5.):

- ◆ Reconfigure the mandates of existing institutions with a view to consolidating institutional links between the Ghana Export Promotion Council, Ghana Free Zone Board and GIPC. This should bring under a single umbrella programme investment promotion in new export-oriented areas such as information technology. Reconfiguration of these institutions and their consolidation in one single agency should be a priority.

- ◆ GIPC should assume the functions of a one-stop centre and help investors to obtain all required authorizations, licenses and permits (including land acquisition) from the authorities concerned. GIPC should also establish investment servicing at the national and regional levels.

- ◆ The AGOA window of opportunity will last for another seven years. GIPC should play a strategic role in spearheading the initiative to take advantage of the privileges provided and to ensure that the appropriate sectoral investment environments are created to attract FDI into the target sectors. Similar action should be taken for the Cotonou Agreement

ANNEX I

Table AI.1 Largest foreign affiliates in Ghana, 1998

(Millions of dollars and numbers)

Company	Home economy	Industry	Sales	Number of employees
A. Industrial				
Unilever Ghana Ltd.	Netherlands/United Kingdom	Diversified	111.06 [a]	1'703 [a]
Teberebie Goldfields Ltd.	United States	Mining	93.20 [a]	1'500 [a]
Pioneer Food Cannery Ltd.	United States	Food	78.50 [a]	1'500 [a]
Volta Aluminium Company Ltd.	United States	Metals and metal products	52.50	1'321
Guinness Ghana Ltd.	Ireland	Beverages	37.90 [a]	180 [a]
Ghana Agro Food Company Ltd.	Germany	Food	35.85 [a]	1'562 [a]
Goldfields (Ghana) Ltd.	South Africa	Mining	17.80 [b]	1'500 [b]
British american Tobacco Company Ltd.	United Kingdom	Tobacco	17.75	400
Wahome Steel Ltd.	Taiwan, Province of China	Metals and metal products	16.40 [a]	527 [a]
Coca-Cola Bottling Company of Ghana Ltd.	United States	Beverages	15.81 [a]	486 [a]
Fan Milk Ghana Ltd.	United States	Food and Beverages	14.33 [a]	379 [a]
Tema Steel Co Ltd	United Kingdom	Metals and metal products	10.53 [a]	584 [a]
Accra Brewery Ltd.	South Africa	Beverages	10.50	430
Bonte Gold Mines Ltd	Canada	Mining	9.73 [a]	320 [a]
Paterson Zochonis Ghana Ltd.	United Kingdom	Chemicals	9.70 [a]	493 [a]
Cadbury Ghana Ltd.	United Kingdom	Beverages	6.40 [a]	255 [a]
Reiss and Co. (Ghana) Ltd.	United Kingdom	Electrical/electronic	5.20 [b]	114 [b]
Ghana Textile Printing Co	Netherlands	Textiles	..	700
Ghana Manganese Company Ltd	United Kingdom	Mining	..	600 [b]
Nestlè Ghana Ltd.	Switzerland	Food and Beverages	..	505 [b]
UEE Explosives (Ghana) Ltd.	Spain	Other manufacturing	..	235
Cluff Mining (West Africa)Ltd.	United Kingdom	Mining	..	230
West African Mining Services Ltd.	Australia	Chemicals	..	220 [b]
Bayswater Contracting & Mining Pty Ltd.	Australia	Mining	..	120 [b]
Ghana Aluminium Products Ltd.	Bermuda	Metals and metal products	..	112 [b]
Everyready Ghana Ltd.	United States	Food	..	100 [b]
Prestea Sankofa Gold Ltd.	United Kingdom	Mining	..	100 [b]
African Star Resources Ltd.	Canada	Mining	..	..
Ausdrill (Ghana) (Pty) Ltd.	Australia	Mining	..	..
Benso Oil Palm Plantation Ltd	United Kingdom	Plantations	..	..
Billiton Bogosu Gold Ltd.	United Kingdom	Mining and metal industry	..	..
Crocodile Matchets (Ghana) Ltd	United Kingdom	Other manufacturing	..	..
Dana Petroleum	United Kingdom	Petroleum	..	..
Ghanaian Australian Goldfields Ltd	Australia	Mining	..	..
Kingsway Chemists of Ghana Ltd.	United Kingdom	Chemicals	..	..
L'air Liquide Ghana Ltd.	France	Chemicals	..	..
Pens & Plastics Ghana	France	Diversified	..	..
Svedala Ghana Ltd.	Sweden	Machinery and equipment	..	..
Swiss Lumber Co Ltd.	Netherlands	Wood and wood products	..	..
Tema Chemicals Ltd.	United Kingdom	Chemicals	..	..

Table AI.1 (contd.) Largest foreign affiliates in Ghana, 1998

(Millions of dollars and numbers)

Company	Home economy	Industry	Sales	Number of employees
B. Tertiary				
Mobil Oil Ghana Ltd.	United States	Distributive Trade	132.30 [a]	125 [a]
Shell Ghana Ltd.	Netherlands/United Kingdom	Distributive Trade	89.30 [a]	123 [a]
Elf Oil Ghana Ltd.	France	Distributive Trade	71.57 [a]	125 [a]
Total Ghana Services Ltd.	France	Distributive Trade	41.06 [a]	34 [a]
Taysec Construction Ltd.	United Kingdom	Construction	39.75 [a]	2'922 [a]
Africa Motors-Division of Tractor & Equipement Ghana Ltd.	Egypt	Distributive Trade	36.20	344
Tema Lube Oil Company	France/United Kingdom	Distributive Trade	17.56 [a]	74 [a]
Novotel Accra	France	Hotels and Restaurants	5.17 [a]	180 [a]
Liner Agencies & Trading (Ghana) Ltd.	United Kingdom	Transport	4.62 [a]	224 [a]
SCOA Ghana Ltd.	France	Motor vehicles	3.88 [a]	140 [a]
Holman Brothers (Ghana) Ltd.	United Kingdom	Machinery and equipment	1.10 [b]	27 [b]
Umarco Ghana Ltd.	Luxembourg	Transport	0.80 [b]	..
Neoplan Ghana	Germany	Motor Vehicles	..	400
CFAO (Ghana) Ltd.	France	Distributive Trade	..	345 [b]
Panalpina Ghana Ltd.	Switzerland	Transport	..	80 [b]
Acg Telesystems (Ghana) Ltd.	United States	Telecommunication	..	75 [b]
Khunesi Coldstres Co	Netherlands	Distributive Trade	..	30 [b]
ECMP Procurement Services	South Africa	Other Services	..	24 [b]
Saikirpa	Netherlands	Distributive Trade	..	10 [b]
Maersk Ghana Ltd.	Denmark	Transport	..	4 [b]
Blackwood Hodge (Ghana) Ltd.	United Kingdom	Distributive Trade	..	..
British Airways	United Kingdom	Transport	..	..
Dizengoff Ghana Ltd.	United Kingdom	Distributive Trade	..	..
Engen Ghana	Malaysia	Distributive Trade	..	..
Ghana Plant Hire Ltd.	United Kingdom	..	..	..
I Kruger Consult AS	France	..	..	..
Interbeton BV	Netherlands	Distributive Trade	..	..
Lapworth Commodities Ltd.	United Kingdom	..	..	..
Rover Ghana Ltd.	United Kingdom	Distributive Trade	..	..
The General Electric Company of Ghana Ltd.	United Kingdom	Distributive Trade	..	..
Taysec Asphalt Ltd.	United Kingdom	Construction	..	..
C. Finance and Insurance			**Assets**	
Standard Chartered Bank Ghana Ltd.	United Kingdom	Banking	390.30	..
Barclays Bank of Ghana Ltd.	United Kingdom	Banking	278.40	594
SSB Bank Ltd.	Switzerland	Banking	261.40	886
Ecobank Ghana Ltd.	Togo	Banking	156.10	205
The Trust Bank Ltd.	Belgium	Banking	37.00	123
Cal Merchant Bank Ltd.	Saudi Arabia	Banking	32.70	140
Crusader Insurance Co (Ghana) Ltd.	United States	Insurance	..	15 [b]
Metropolitan Insurance Company Ltd	India	Insurance	..	6 [b]
Central Finance Co Ltd.	United Kingdom	Banking	..	..

Source: : UNCTAD (forthcoming). Transfer of Technology Policies – Case Studies of Ghana, Kenya, Tanzania and Uganda.

ANNEX II

UNCTAD/EMPRETEC GHANA survey on small and medium-sized firms in Ghana

UNCTAD, in collaboration with EMPRETEC Ghana, conducted a survey in 2001 of small and medium-sized enterprises (SMEs) in Ghana having linkages with a foreign firm, to identify the benefits of such linkages and opportunities to increase their benefits. Linkages have been defined as backward (acquiring goods or services from local firms), forward (foreign firms selling goods or service to local firms), or horizontal (interaction with foreign firms engaged in competing activities). The survey was based on a mailed questionnaire and interviews with 50 enterprises

1. Profile of the surveyed companies

Of the 50 enterprises surveyed, 18 per cent were in services, 62 per cent were manufacturers and 20 per cent were in agriculture. The selection criterion for the sample was the existence of a linkage between a local and a foreign firm. In the firm sample, business areas covered garment manufacturing, manufacturing of aluminium products, handicrafts and carvings, furniture and citrus production, shea butter production, and trading. In terms of ownership, 28 per cent of the enterprises are owned by individuals, 44 per cent are family-owned and 20 per cent are partnerships between Ghanaians. The remainder have full foreign ownership.

Table AII. I. Ownership structure

(Percentage)

Ownership	Number	Percentage
Owned by individual	14	28
Family-owned	22	44
Partnerships of locals	10	20
Foreign affiliate	3	6
Partnership with foreign firm	1	2
TOTAL	50	100

Most of the enterprises surveyed (44%) were established in the 1990s. Firm size had increased significantly in the past five years (table AII.2). Whereas in 1995 only one-third of the firms sampled employed more than 20 people, this had increased to almost three-quarters by 2000.

Table AII. 2. Employment generation in sample firms, 1995-2000

(Percentage)

Number of employees	In 1995 or year of establishment	In 2000
1 – 5	30	6
6 – 20	38	26
21 – 50	16	28
51 – 100	4	22
101 – 150	6	8
151 and above	6	10

85

Of the firms in the sample, 88 per cent are exporters, while 50 per cent of the firms surveyed started exporting after 1995. The most popular export destination is Europe (54 per cent), followed by the United States (38 per cent) and West Africa (30 per cent). In the sample, 66 per cent of firms are suppliers of TNCs and 78 per cent import machinery or raw materials from foreign firms.

2. Importance of linkages

Foreign firms - according to the majority of respondents - provided critical support to the business, among the factors cited most important are product improvement and training.

Figure AII.1. Support received by foreign companies in business development

(Percentage of firms citing "important" or "very important" for individual factors)

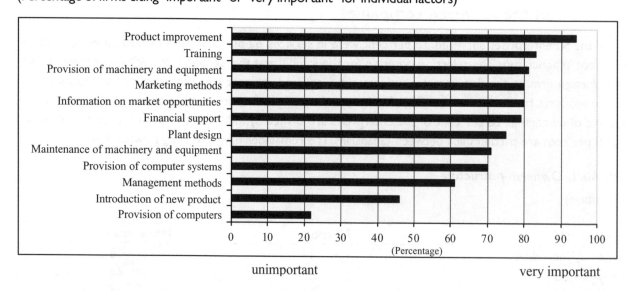

From the point of view of the local partner, the quality of services local firms are able to provide to foreign businesses and the knowledge of the local market are critical in their relationship with foreign firms. In the interviews and in open questions, firms also quoted "building trust", as a critical factor for establishing and promoting linkages.

Figure AII.2. Mean ranking of factors important in the relation between foreign firms and local firms in Ghana

(Rating from 1 = "unimportant" to 4= "very important")

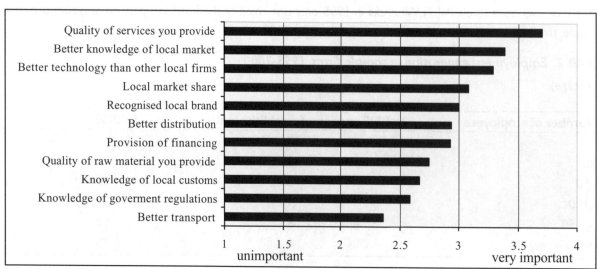

3. Bottlenecks in business operations

Most of the respondents suggested they would benefit from closer relationships with foreign firms and ranked areas for improvement as follows: exports, marketing, credit, technology, labour skills and product improvement. Firms surveyed expressed general dissatisfaction with the prevailing business environment. When survey respondents were asked to rate areas where they encounter problems in their business operations, all factors listed ranked above average, pointing to supply constraints as well as difficulties related to marketing and distribution (figure AII.4). The most cited bottlenecks identified by the respondents in open questions were lack of finance (40 per cent), followed by lack of export facilitation. Other factors listed included high taxes/import duties, lack of skilled labour, marketing, high cost of utilities, problems related to land acquisition, lack of fiscal incentives and lack/low quality of local materials.

Figure AII.3. Mean ranking for areas in which companies need improvement

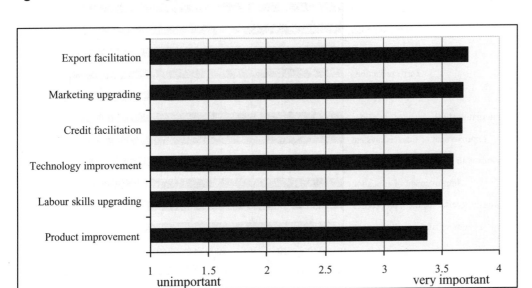

Figure AII.4. Mean ranking for satisfaction with current incentives provided to firms

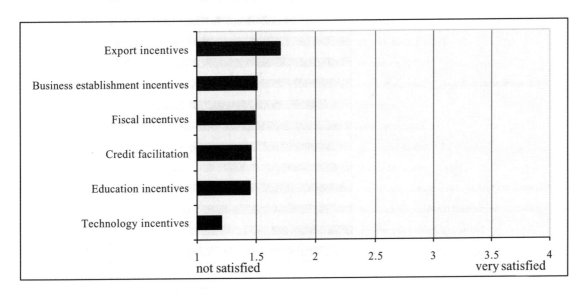

The responses about the adequacy of investment incentives are more meaningfully represented as a dissatisfaction index. All incentives currently offered to firms were generally rated ineffective by the respondents. Technology and education were identified as most inadequate by respondents (figure AII.4).

4. Suggested policy improvements

When asked about measures that would best help to expand their businesses, better access to credit was considered to be the most important followed by export promotion. Enterprises operating in service industries responded that export promotion (78 per cent of respondents) would best help in expanding their businesses. In the case of firms with foreign ownership the rating was different: improvement in the area of training was considered the most important.

Figure AII.5. Which of these measures would best help in expanding your business?

(Percentage of firms citing "important" or "very important" for individual factors")

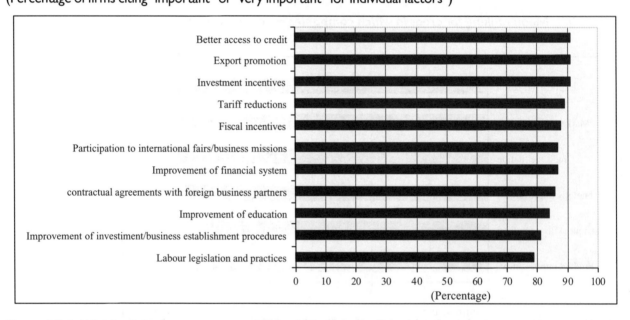

Figure AII.6. Which of these measures would best help in expanding your business?

(Per cent of firms with foreign ownership citing "important" or "very important" for individual factors)

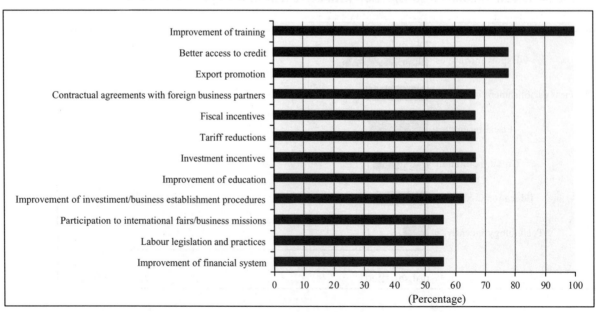

Selected UNCTAD publications on transnational corporations and foreign direct investment

(For more information, please visit www.unctad.org/en/pub)

A. Serial publications

World Investment Reports

World Investment Report 2001: Promoting Linkages. 356 p. Sales N°. E.01.II.D.12 $49. http://www.unctad.org/wir/contents/wir01content.en.htm.

World Investment Report 2001: Promoting Linkage. *An Overview*. 67 p. Free of charge. http://www.unctad.org/wir/contents/wir01content.en.htm.

Ten Years of World Investment Reports: The Challenges Ahead. *Proceedings of an UNCTAD special event on future challenges in the area of FDI*. UNCTAD/ITE/Misc.45. Free of charge. http://www.unctad.org/wir.

World Investment Report 2000: Cross-border Mergers and Acquisitions and Development. 368 p. Sales N°. E.99.II.D.20. $49. http://www.unctad.org/wir/contents/wir00content.en.htm.

World Investment Report 2000: Cross-border Mergers and Acquisitions and Development. *An Overview* . 75 p. Free of charge. http://www.unctad.org/wir/contents/wir00content.en.htm

World Investment Report 1999: Foreign Direct Investment and the Challenge of Development. 543 p. Sales N°. E.99.II.D.3. $49. http://www.unctad.org/wir/contents/wir99content.en.htm.

World Investment Report 1999: Foreign Direct Investment and Challenge of Development. *An Overview* . 75 p. Free of charge. http://www.unctad.org/wir/contents/wir99content.en.htm

World Investment Report 1998: Trends and Determinants. 432 p. Sales No. E.98.II.D.5. $45. http://www.unctad.org/wir/contents/wir98content.en.htm.

World Investment Report 1998: Trends and Determinants. *An Overview*. 67 p. Free of charge. http://www.unctad.org/wir/contents/wir98content.en.htm.

World Investment Report 1997: Transnational Corporations, Market Structure and Competition Policy. 384 p. Sales N°. E.97.II.D.10. $45. http://www.unctad.org/wir/contents/wir97content.en.htm.

World Investment Report 1997: Transnational Corporations, Market Structure and Competition Policy. *An Overview*. 70 p. Free of charge. http://www.unctad.org/wir/contents/wir97content.en.htm.

World Investment Report 1996: Investment, Trade and International Policy Arrangements. 332 p. Sales N°. E.96.II.A.14. $45. http://www.unctad.org/wir/contents/wir96content.en.htm.

World Investment Report 1996: Investment, Trade and International Policy Arrangements. *An Overview*. 51 p. Free of charge. http://www.unctad.org/wir/contents/wir96content.en.htm.

World Investment Report 1995: Transnational Corporations and Competitiveness. 491 p. Sales N°. E.95.II.A.9. $45. http://www.unctad.org/wir/contents/wir95content.en.htm.

World Investment Report 1995: Transnational Corporations and Competitiveness. An Overview . 51 p. Free of charge. http://www.unctad.org/wir/contents/wir95content.en.htm

World Investment Report 1994: Transnational Corporations, Employment and the Workplace. 482 p. Sales N°. E.94.II.A.14. $45. http://www.unctad.org/wir/contents/wir94content.en.htm.

World Investment Report 1994: Transnational Corporations, Employment and the Workplace. An Executive Summary . 34 p. http://www.unctad.org/wir/contents/wir94content.en.htm

World Investment Report 1993: Transnational Corporations and Integrated International Production. 290 p. Sales N°. E.93.II.A.14. $45. http://www.unctad.org/wir/contents/wir93content.en.htm.

World Investment Report 1993: Transnational Corporations and Integrated International Production. An Executive Summary. 31 p. ST/CTC/159. Free of charge. http://www.unctad.org/wir/contents/wir93content.en.htm.

World Investment Report 1992: Transnational Corporations as Engines of Growth. 356 p. Sales N°. E.92.II.A.19. $45. http://www.unctad.org/wir/contents/wir92content.en.htm.

World Investment Report 1992: Transnational Corporations as Engines of Growth. An Executive Summary . 30 p. Sales N°. E.92.II.A.24. Free of charge. http://www.unctad.org/wir/contents/wir92content.en.htm.

World Investment Report 1991: The Triad in Foreign Direct Investment. 108 p. Sales N°.E.91.II.A.12. $25. http://www.unctad.org/wir/contents/wir91content.en.htm.

World Investment Directories

World Investment Directory 1999: Asia and the Pacific. Vol. VII (Parts I and II). 332+638 p. Sales N°. E.00.II.D.21. $80.

World Investment Directory 1996: West Asia . Vol. VI. 138 p. Sales N°. E.97.II.A.2. $35.

World Investment Directory 1996: Africa. Vol. V. 461 p. Sales N°. E.97.II.A.1. $75.

World Investment Directory 1994: Latin America and the Caribbean. Vol. IV. 478 p. Sales N°. E.94.II.A.10. $65.

World Investment Directory 1992: Developed Countries. Vol. III. 532 p. Sales N°. E.93.II.A.9. $75.

World Investment Directory 1992: Central and Eastern Europe. Vol. II. 432 p. Sales N°. E.93.II.A.1. $65. (Joint publication with the United Nations Economic Commission for Europe.)

World Investment Directory 1992: Asia and the Pacific. Vol. I. 356 p. Sales N°. E.92.II.A.11. $65.

Investment Policy Reviews

Investment Policy Review of the United Republic of Tanzania. 98 p. Sales N°. 02.E.II.D.6 $ 20. http://www.unctad.org/en/docs/poiteipcm9.en.pdf.

Investment Policy Review of Ecuador. 117 p. Sales N°. E.01.II D.31. $ 25. Summary available from http://www.unctad.org/en/docs/poiteipcm2sum.en.pdf.

Investment and Innovation Policy Review of Ethiopia. 115 p. UNCTAD/ITE/IPC/Misc.4. Free of charge. http://www.unctad.org/en/docs/poiteipcm4.en.pdf.

Investment Policy Review of Mauritius. 84 p. Sales N°. E.01.II.D.11. $22. Summary available from http://www.unctad.org/en/pub/investpolicy.en.htm.

Investment Policy Review of Peru. 108 p. Sales N°. E.00.II.D. 7. $22. Summary available from http://www.unctad.org/en/docs/poiteiipm19sum.en.pdf.

Investment Policy Review of Uganda. 75 p. Sales N°. E.99.II.D.24. $15. Summary available from http://www.unctad.org/en/docs/poiteiipm17sum.en.Pdf.

Investment Policy Review of Egypt. 113 p. Sales N°. E.99.II.D.20. $19. Summary available from http://www.unctad.org/en/docs/poiteiipm11sum.en.Pdf.

Investment Policy Review of Uzbekistan. 64 p. UNCTAD/ITE/IIP/Misc.13. Free of charge. http://www.unctad.org/en/docs/poiteiipm13.en.pdf.

International Investment Instruments

International Investment Instruments: A Compendium. Vol. IX. 353 p. Sales N°. E.02.II.D.16. $60. http://www.unctad.org/en/docs/psdited3v9.en.pdf.

International Investment Instruments: A Compendium. Vol. VIII. 335 p. Sales N°. E.02.II.D.15. $60. http://www.unctad.org/en/docs/psdited3v8.en.pdf.

International Investment Instruments: A Compendium. Vol. VII. 339 p. Sales N°. E.02.II.D.14. $60. http://www.unctad.org/en/docs/psdited3v7.en.pdf.

International Investment Instruments: A Compendium. Vol. VI. 568 p. Sales N°. E.01.II.D.34. $60. http://www.unctad.org/en/docs/ps1dited2v6_p1.en.pdf (part one).

International Investment Instruments: A Compendium. Vol. V. 505 p. Sales N°. E.00.II.D.14. $55.

International Investment Instruments: A Compendium. Vol. IV. 319 p. Sales N°. E.00.II.D.13. $55.

International Investment Instruments: A Compendium. Vol. I. 371 p. Sales N°. E.96.II.A.9; *Vol. II.* 577 p. Sales N°. E.96.II.A.10; *Vol. III.* 389 p. Sales N°. E.96.II.A.11; **the 3-volume set**, Sales N°. E.96.II.A.12. $125.

Bilateral Investment Treaties 1959-1999. 143 p. UNCTAD/ITE/IIA/2, Free of charge. Available only in electronic version from http://www.unctad.org/en/pub/poiteiiad2.en.htm.

Bilateral Investment Treaties in the Mid-1990s. 314 p. Sales N°. E.98.II.D.8. $46.

LDC Investment Guides

An Investment Guide to Mozambique: Opportunities and Conditions. 72 p. UNCTAD/ITE/IIA/4. http://www.unctad.org/en/pub/investguide.en.htm

An Investment Guide to Uganda: Opportunities and Conditions. 76 p. UNCTAD/ITE/IIT/Misc.30. http://www.unctad.org/en/docs/poiteiitm30.en.pdf.

An Investment Guide to Bangladesh: Opportunities and Conditions. 66 p. UNCTAD/ITE/IIT/Misc.29. http://www.unctad.org/en/docs/poiteiitm29.en.pdf.

Guide d'investissement au Mali. 108 p. UNCTAD/ITE/IIT/Misc.24. http://www.unctad.org/fr/docs/poiteiitm24.fr.pdf. (Joint publication with the International Chamber of Commerce, in association with PricewaterhouseCoopers.)

An Investment Guide to Ethiopia: Opportunities and Conditions. 69 p. UNCTAD/ITE/IIT/Misc.19. http://www.unctad.org/en/docs/poiteiitm19.en.pdf. (Joint publication with the International Chamber of Commerce, in association with PricewaterhouseCoopers.)

Issues in International Investment Agreements
(Executive summaries are available from http://www.unctad.org/iia.)

Transfer of Technology. 138 p. Sales N°. E.01.II.D.33. $18.

Illicit Payments. 108 p. Sales N°. E.01.II.D.20. $13.

Home Country Measures. 96 p. Sales N°.E.01.II.D.19. $12.

Host Country Operational Measures. 109 p. Sales N° E.01.II.D.18. $15.

Social Responsibility. 91 p. Sales N°. E.01.II.D.4. $15.

Environment. 105 p. Sales N°. E.01.II.D.3. $15.

Transfer of Funds. 68 p. Sales N°. E.00.II.D.27. $12.

Employment. 69 p. Sales N°. E.00.II.D.15. $12.

Taxation. 111 p. Sales N°. E.00.II.D.5. $12.

International Investment Agreements: Flexibility for Development. 185 p. Sales N°. E.00.II.D.6. $12.

Taking of Property. 83 p. Sales N°. E.00.II.D.4. $12.

Trends in International Investment Agreements: An Overview. 112 p. Sales N°. E.99.II.D.23. $ 12.

Lessons from the MAI. 31 p. Sales N°. E.99.II.D.26. $ 12.

National Treatment. 104 p. Sales N°. E.99.II.D.16. $12.

Fair and Equitable Treatment. 64 p. Sales N°. E.99.II.D.15. $12.

Investment-Related Trade Measures. 64 p. Sales N°. E.99.II.D.12. $12.

Most-Favoured-Nation Treatment. 72 p. Sales N°. E.99.II.D.11. $12.

Admission and Establishment. 72 p. Sales N°. E.99.II.D.10. $12.

Scope and Definition. 96 p. Sales N°. E.99.II.D.9. $12.

Transfer Pricing. 72 p. Sales N°. E.99.II.D.8. $12.

Foreign Direct Investment and Development. 88 p. Sales N°. E.98.II.D.15. $12.

B. Current Studies
Series A

N°. 30. *Incentives and Foreign Direct Investment.* 98 p. Sales N°. E.96.II.A.6. $30. [Out of print.]

N°. 29. *Foreign Direct Investment, Trade, Aid and Migration.* 100 p. Sales N°. E.96.II.A.8. $25. (Joint publication with the International Organization for Migration.)

N°. 28. *Foreign Direct Investment in Africa.* 119 p. Sales N°. E.95.II.A.6. $20.

ASIT Advisory Studies (Formerly Current Studies, Series B)

N°. 17. *The World of Investment Promotion at a Glance: A survey of investment promotion practices.* UNCTAD/ITE/IPC/3. Free of charge.

N°. 16. *Tax Incentives and Foreign Direct Investment: A Global Survey.* 180 p. Sales N°. E.01.II.D.5. $23. Summary available from http://www.unctad.org/asit/resumÈ.htm

N°. 15. *Investment Regimes in the Arab World: Issues and Policies.* 232 p. Sales N°. E/F.00.II.D.32.

N°. 14. *Handbook on Outward Investment Promotion Agencies and Institutions.* 50 p. Sales N°. E.99.II.D.22. $ 15.

N°. 13. *Survey of Best Practices in Investment Promotion.* 71 p. Sales N°. E.97.II.D.11. $ 35.

N°. 12. *Comparative Analysis of Petroleum Exploration Contracts.* 80 p. Sales N°. E.96.II.A.7. $35.

N°. 11. *Administration of Fiscal Regimes for Petroleum Exploration and Development.* 45 p. Sales N°. E.95.II.A.8.

C. Individual Studies

The Tradability of Consulting Services. 189 p. UNCTAD/ITE/IPC/Misc.8.
http://www.unctad.org/en/docs/poiteipcm8.en.pdf.

Compendium of International Arrangements on Transfer of Technology: Selected Instruments.
308 p. Sales N°. E.01.II.D.28. $45.

FDI in Least Developed Countries at a Glance. 150 p. UNCTAD/ITE/IIA/3. Free of charge. Also
available from http://www.unctad.org/en/pub/poiteiiad3.en.htm.

Foreign Direct Investment in Africa: Performance and Potential. 89 p.
UNCTAD/ITE/IIT/Misc.15. Free of charge. Also available from
http://www.unctad.org/en/docs/poiteiitm15.pdf.

TNC-SME Linkages for Development: Issues-Experiences-Best Practices. *Proceedings of the
Special Round Table on TNCs, SMEs and Development, UNCTAD X, 15 February 2000,
Bangkok, Thailand.* 113 p. UNCTAD/ITE/TEB1. Free of charge.

*Handbook on Foreign Direct Investment by Small and Medium-sized Enterprises: Lessons
from Asia*. 200 p. Sales N°. E.98.II.D.4. $48.

*Handbook on Foreign Direct Investment by Small and Medium-sized Enterprises: Lessons
from Asia*. *Executive Summary and Report of the Kunming Conference*. 74 p. Free of charge.

Small and Medium-sized Transnational Corporations. *Executive Summary and Report of the
Osaka Conference*. 60 p. Free of charge.

Small and Medium-sized Transnational Corporations: Role, Impact and Policy Implications.
242 p. Sales N°. E.93.II.A.15. $35.

Measures of the Transnationalization of Economic Activity. 93 p. Sales N°. E.01.II.D.2. $20.

*The Competitiveness Challenge: Transnational Corporations and Industrial Restructuring in
Developing Countries*. 283p. Sales N°. E.00.II.D.35. $42.

Integrating International and Financial Performance at the Enterprise Level. 116 p.
Sales N°. E.00.II.D.28. $18.

FDI Determinants and TNCs Strategies: The Case of Brazil. 195 p. Sales N°. E.00.II.D.2. $35.
Summary available from http://www.unctad.org/en/pub/psiteiitd14.en.htm.

The Social Responsibility of Transnational Corporations. 75 p. UNCTAD/ITE/IIT/Misc. 21. Free
of charge. [Out of stock.] Available from http://www.unctad.org/en/docs/poiteiitm21.en.pdf.

Conclusions on Accounting and Reporting by Transnational Corporations. 47 p.
Sales N°. E.94.II.A.9. $25.

Accounting, Valuation and Privatization. 190 p. Sales N°. E.94.II.A.3. $25.

*Environmental Management in Transnational Corporations: Report on the Benchmark
Corporate Environment Survey*. 278 p. Sales N°. E.94.II.A.2. $29.95.

Management Consulting: A Survey of the Industry and Its Largest Firms. 100 p. Sales N°. E.93.II.A.17. $25.

Transnational Corporations: A Selective Bibliography, 1991-1992. 736 p. Sales N°. E.93.II.A.16. $75.

Foreign Investment and Trade Linkages in Developing Countries. 108 p. Sales N°. E.93.II.A.12. $18.

Transnational Corporations from Developing Countries: Impact on Their Home Countries. 116 p. Sales N°. E.93.II.A.8. $15.

Debt-Equity Swaps and Development. 150 p. Sales N°. E.93.II.A.7. $35.

From the Common Market to EC 92: Regional Economic Integration in the European Community and Transnational Corporations. 134 p. Sales N°. E.93.II.A.2. $25.

The East-West Business Directory 1991/1992. 570 p. Sales N°. E.92.II.A.20. $65.

Climate Change and Transnational Corporations: Analysis and Trends. 110 p. Sales N°. E.92.II.A.7. $16.50.

Foreign Direct Investment and Transfer of Technology in India. 150 p. Sales N°. E.92.II.A.3. $20.

The Determinants of Foreign Direct Investment: A Survey of the Evidence. 84 p. Sales N°. E.92.II.A.2. $12.50.

Transnational Corporations and Industrial Hazards Disclosure. 98 p. Sales N°. E.91.II.A.18. $17.50.

Transnational Business Information: A Manual of Needs and Sources. 216 p. Sales N°. E.91.II.A.13. $45.

The Financial Crisis in Asia and Foreign Direct Investment: An Assessment. 101 p. Sales N°. GV.E.98.0.29. $20.

Sharing Asiaís Dynamism: Asian Direct Investment in the European Union. 192 p. Sales N°. E.97.II.D.1. $26.

Investing in Asiaís Dynamism: European Union Direct Investment in Asia. 124 p. ISBN 92-827-7675-1. ECU 14. (Joint publication with the European Commission.)

International Investment towards the Year 2002. 166 p. Sales N°. GV.E.98.0.15. $29. (Joint publication with Invest in France Mission and Arthur Andersen, in collaboration with DATAR.)

International Investment towards the Year 2001. 81 p. Sales N°. GV.E.97.0.5. $35. (Joint publication with Invest in France Mission and Arthur Andersen, in collaboration with DATAR.)

D. Journals

Transnational Corporations Journal (formerly ***The CTC Reporter***). Published three times a year. Annual subscription price: $45; individual issues $20.
http://www.unctad.org/en/subsites/dite/1_itncs/1_tncs.htm

United Nations publications may be obtained from bookstores and distributors throughout the world. Please consult your bookstore or write to:

For Africa, Asia and Europe to:

Sales Section
United Nations Office at Geneva
Palais des Nations
CH-1211 Geneva 10
Switzerland
Tel: (41-22) 917-1234
Fax: (41-22) 917-0123
E-mail: unpubli@unog.ch

For Asia and the Pacific, the Caribbean, Latin America and North America to:

Sales Section
Room DC2-0853
United Nations Secretariat
New York, NY 10017
United States
Tel: (1-212) 963-8302 or (800) 253-9646
Fax: (1-212) 963-3489
E-mail: publications@un.org

All prices are quoted in United States dollars.

For further information on the work of the Division on Investment, Technology and Enterprise Development, UNCTAD, please address inquiries to:
United Nations Conference on Trade and Development
Division on Investment, Technology and Enterprise Development
Palais des Nations, Room E-10054
CH-1211 Geneva 10, Switzerland
Telephone: (41-22) 907-5651
Telefax: (41-22) 907-0498
E-mail: natalia.guerra@unctad.org

READERSHIP SURVEY

Investment Policy Review of Ghana

In order to improve the quality and relevance of the work of the UNCTAD Division on Investment, Technology and Enterprise Development, it would be useful to receive the views of readers on this and other similar publications. It would therefore be greatly appreciated if you could complete the following questionnaire and return it to:

Readership Survey
UNCTAD, Division on Investment, Technology and Enterprise Development
United Nations Office in Geneva
Palais des Nations
Room E-10074
CH-1211 Geneva 10
Switzerland
Or by Fax to: 41-22-9070197

> This questionnaire is also available to be filled out on line at: www.unctad.org/ipr

1.   Name **and professional** address of respondent (optional):

_____

_____

2.   Which of the following best describes your area of work?

Government ☐   Public enterprise ☐
Private enterprise institution ☐   Academic or research ☐
International organization ☐   Media ☐
Not-for-profit organization ☐   Other (specify) ☐

3.   In which country do you work?   _____

4.   What is your assessment of the contents of this publication?

Excellent ☐   Adequate ☐
Good ☐   Poor ☐

5.   How useful is this publication to your work?

Very useful ☐   Of some use ☐   Irrelevant ☐

6.   Please indicate the three things you liked best about this publication **and are useful to your work**:

_____

_____

7. Please indicate the three things you liked least about this publication:

    _____

    _____

    _____

8. If you have read more than the present publication of the UNCTAD Division on Investment, Enterprise Development and Technology, what is your overall assessment of them?

    Consistently good ☐   Usually good, but with some exceptions ☐

    Generally mediocre ☐   Poor ☐

9. On the average, how useful are these publications to you in your work?

    Very useful ☐   Of some use ☐   Irrelevant ☐

10. Are you a regular recipient of Transnational Corporations (formerly The CTC Reporter), the Division's tri-annual refereed journal?

    Yes ☐   No ☐

    If not, please check here if you would like to receive a sample copy sent to the name and address you have given above. Other titles you would like to receive instead (seelist of publications).

    _____

    _____

    _____

11. How or where did you get this publication:

    I bought it ☐   In a seminar/workshop ☐

    I requested a courtesy copy ☐   Direct mailing ☐

    Other ☐

12. Would you like to receive information on the work of UNCTAD in the area of Investment Technology and Enterprise Development through e-mail ? If yes, please write your e-mail address below:

    _____

Printed at United Nations, Geneva
GE.03-51268–June 2003–3,240

UNCTAD/ITE/IPC/MISC.14

United Nations publication
Sales No. E.02.II.D.20

ISBN 92-1-112569-3